CRUISE SHIPS OF THE MERSEY
Ian Collard

First pubished April 2016 by
Bernard McCall, 400 Nore Road, Portishead, Bristol, BS20 8EZ, England.
Tel: +44 (0) 1275 846178
email: bernard@coastalshipping.co.uk. website: www.coastalshipping.co.uk
Design: Sarah Baber

ISBN 978-1-90295-376-2

Printed by : (G) Gomer Press, Llandysul Enterprise Park, Llandysul, Ceredigion, WALES, SA44 4JL.
Telephone : +44 (0) 1559 362371   Fax : +44 (0) 1559 363758
email : sales@gomer.co.uk   website : www.gomerprinting.co.uk

FRONT COVER

Ocean Monarch 1956 25,585 gt. 182.8 x 25.9 x 14.6m.   20 knots.

b. Vickers Armstrong (Shipbuilders), Walker on Tyne, Newcastle. Yard No 155.   IMO 5103948.

Shaw, Savill & Albion Line

Ocean Monarch is assisted by the Rea tug *Willowgarth* in Langton Dock as she moves to Princes Landing Stage to embark passengers, following her acquisition by the Shaw, Savill & Albion Line.

She was built as *Empress of England* for the Canadian Pacific Steamship Company and was launched by Lady Eden, wife of the British Prime Minister, on 9 May 1956. *Empress of England* was employed on Canadian Pacific's Liverpool to Canada service, and cruising in the winter months. She was chartered to the Travel Savings Association in 1963, operating on cruises from Cape Town. The following year she was returned to Canadian Pacific who sold her to Shaw, Savill & Albion in 1970, and she was renamed *Ocean Monarch*. She left Southampton for Australia on 5 November and was employed on a series of cruises out of Sydney. However, following a series of mechanical breakdowns in 1974, she returned to the United Kingdom. *Ocean Monarch* was sold to ship breakers the following year and left Southampton in June, 1975 for Kaohsiung, where she was broken up.

REAR COVER

A view from the *Queen Mary 2* as she approaches the Three Graces, Liverpool - from left to right, the Royal Liver Building, the Cunard Building and the former offices of the Mersey Docks and Harbour Board.

Brochure 1 — Liverpool & North Wales Steamship Company

THE LIVERPOOL & NORTH WALES STEAMSHIP COMPANY LTD.

SAILINGS FROM LLANDUDNO
(Sundays included)

WHITSUNTIDE to SEPTEMBER
(Weather and other circumstances permitting)

"ST. TUDNO" or "ST. SEIRIOL"

		Due Return Back	Fare
Daily 1-15 p.m.	For MENAI BRIDGE (One hour ashore)	5-0 p.m.	6/-
Tuesdays 10-15 a.m.	For DOUGLAS (I.o.M.) (Three hours ashore) (Extra Sailing Wednesdays July and August)	7-50 p.m.	17/-
Certain Wednesdays 9-30 a.m.	To LIVERPOOL (Two hours ashore)	4-30 p.m.	7/6
Sundays! 2-45 p.m.	ANGLESEY COAST CRUISE TO RED WHARF & BENLLECH BAYS	4-45 p.m.	4/-

M. V. "ST. TRILLO"

10-45 a.m.	MORNING CRUISE	12-30 p.m.	3/-
2-30 p.m.	CRUISE TO MENAI BRIDGE	6-0 p.m.	6/-
7-30 p.m.	EVENING CRUISE (Suns. Mons. and Weds.)	9-0 p.m.	3/-

SAILINGS FROM MENAI BRIDGE

M. V. "ST. TRILLO"

		Due Return Back	Fare
Suns. Weds. and Fridays 9-0 a.m.	To LLANDUDNO (4 hours ashore)	4-0 p.m.	6/-
Tuesdays and Thursdays 12-30 p.m.	To LLANDUDNO (4 hours ashore)	8-0 p.m.	6/-

"ST. TUDNO" or "ST. SEIRIOL"

			Fare
Daily 3-45 p.m.	To LLANDUDNO (Single Journey)	Due 5-0 p.m.	4/6

For particulars of Circular Tours outward by Steamer returning by Bus or Train See Bills

Weekly Cruise Tickets (Monday to Saturday) Issued at Pier Gates Office. Available All Advertised Sailings, 20/-

Through Rail Bookings from Prestatyn, Rhyl, Abergele, Old Colwyn, Llandudno Junction, Llanfairfechan, Penmaenmawr and Bangor in connection with all sailings

All tickets are issued, passengers and goods carried subject to the Company's Conditions of Carriage, as exhibited at the Company's Offices and on the vessels

For all further particulars apply at Company's Office, Pier Gates, Llandudno (Tel. 6837), Pier Gates, Menai Bridge (Tel. 12) or The Liverpool and North Wales Steamship Co. Ltd., 40 Chapel Street, Liverpool (Tel. CENtral 1653)

Brochure 2 — Manchester Ship Canal

TIME TABLE

Special cruise along the full length of the

MANCHESTER SHIP CANAL

aboard the T.S.M.V. 'Egremont'
Saturday, 13th May, 1972

Saturday, 13th May,

08-30 hours. Embarkation commences in T.S.M.V. 'Egremont' Pomona Docks—Cornbrook Road entrance, off Chester Road, Manchester.

09-00 hours. On completion of embarkation, T.S.M.V. 'Egremont' leaves for New Brighton via the Manchester Ship Canal and Mersey Estuary. (Please see map and historical note.)

16-00 hours (approx.). Due to arrive Liverpool.

There is a frequent service of trains from Liverpool (Lime Street) Station) to Manchester, and the following are considered to be the most suitable, but passengers may return by any train they desire.

Liverpool depart	17-05	17-35	18-10	18-35	19-35	20-30
Piccadilly arrive	—	18-29	—	19-26	20-27	—
Victoria arrive	17-47	—	18-56	—	—	21-16

A BUFFET will be available in the T.S.M.V. 'Egremont' during the journey for the sale of light refreshments.

Co-op Travel gives notice that all the arrangements shown on this programme are made by them as agents only. All tickets issued by them for conveyance by rail or steamboat or other mode of carriage of any sort over advertised routes are issued by them as agents for the companies or proprietors or others advertising such routes. In all other cases arrangements are made by them as agents for the passengers. Co-op Travel cannot under any circumstances accept any liability for loss, delay, accident, or irregularity which may be caused by neglect or default of any company or person concerned in the carrying out of these arrangements who is not in its actual employment.

Issued by Co-op Travel
Corporation Street, Manchester, M60 4ES

co-op Travel

Brochure 3 — Coastal Cruising Association

COASTAL CRUISING ASSOCIATION

SPECIAL SPRING CRUISE

Liverpool and North Wales
(LLANDUDNO AND MENAI BRIDGE)
SATURDAY 15th MAY 1971

by M.V. BALMORAL

Depart from		Return time
LIVERPOOL (Princes Stage)	10 00	20 30
LLANDUDNO	13 15	17 30
MENAI BRIDGE	14 30	16 00

Thence cruise passing under Menai Suspension Bridge and Britannia Railway Bridge and viewing Port Dinorwic. Cruise departs Menai Bridge 14 45 and returns 15 45.

DAY RETURN FARES:	Booked in Advance	Booked on day
From LIVERPOOL to LLANDUDNO	£1.50	£1.75
From LIVERPOOL to MENAI BRIDGE	£2.00	£2.25
From LIVERPOOL to MENAI STRAITS CRUISE	£2.25	£2.50
From LLANDUDNO to MENAI BRIDGE	80p	80p
From LLANDUDNO to MENAI STRAITS CRUISE	£1.10	£1.10
CRUISE from MENAI BRIDGE	50p	50p

Children 3-14 years half fare

Please note Special Advance Fares for tickets purchased prior to day of sailing Advance Booking strongly advised (Fares refunded if sailing cancelled)

BOOKING ARRANGEMENTS
Tickets for the cruise and meals during voyage may be purchased by post only from:— M. R. McRonald, 48 Wellington Road, Birkenhead, L43 2JF

Steamer tickets may also be purchased alongside the ship on 15th May (subject to availability) or in advance from:—

Vintage brochures advertising cruises that start from or visit the River Mersey.

Brochure 4 — Day Cruise

It's a WONDERFUL day out on a . . .

DAY CRUISE to LLANDUDNO and MENAI BRIDGE aboard ST. TUDNO and ST. SEIRIOL

The LIVERPOOL & NORTH WALES STEAMSHIP CO. LTD.
40 CHAPEL STREET · LIVERPOOL · 3 · CENtral 1653

Brochure 5 — Cunard White Star

SEA AND SUN-BATHING AT THE "HOMERIC'S" LIDO

Come Cruising!

No matter at what time of the year—spring, summer autumn or winter—you will always be able to find a Cunard White Star cruise to suit. Between Christmas and next autumn there is a choice of thirty delightful cruises to colourful ports in the Mediterranean, West Indies, Atlantic Isles and Norway by the magnificent cruising liners "Homeric," "Laconia," "Lancastria" "Doric" and "Laurentic"

From £7 One Class Only

Full details of the itineraries will be found in the booklet

Cunard White Star

Brochure 6 — The Royal Iris

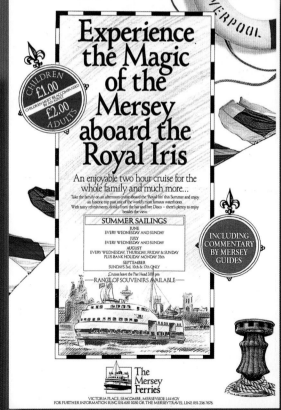

CHILDREN £1.00 (CHILDREN MUST BE ACCOMPANIED BY AN ADULT) £2.00 ADULTS

Experience the Magic of the Mersey aboard the Royal Iris

An enjoyable two hour cruise for the whole family and much more...

Take the family on an afternoon cruise aboard the Royal Iris this Summer and enjoy an historic trip past one of the world's most famous waterfronts. With tasty refreshments, drinks from the bar and free Disco — there's plenty to enjoy besides on the cruise.

INCLUDING COMMENTARY BY MERSEY GUIDES

SUMMER SAILINGS
JUNE EVERY WEDNESDAY AND SUNDAY
JULY EVERY WEDNESDAY AND SUNDAY
AUGUST EVERY WEDNESDAY, THURSDAY, FRIDAY & SUNDAY PLUS BANK HOLIDAY MONDAY 28th
SEPTEMBER SUNDAYS 3rd, 10th & 17th ONLY

Cruises leave the Pier Head 3.00 pm

RANGE OF SOUVENIRS AVAILABLE

The Mersey Ferries

VICTORIA PLACE, SEACOMBE, MERSEYSIDE L44 6QY
FOR FURTHER INFORMATION RING 051-630 1030 OR THE MERSEYTRAVEL LINE 051-236 7676

For the many thousands of cruise passengers that use the River Mersey, and in 2014 forty seven vessels and 54,595 of those passengers docked at Pier Head, and for the many more who like to look at the ships and want to find out more about them, this book is for you. It provides an overview of visiting cruise ships from the 1930s to the present day. Each photograph is accompanied by a history of the ship, its specifications and ownership. **Cruise Ships of the Mersey** is meant as an introduction or taster, if you like, and I hope that by sharing my lifelong passion readers will use this book as a springboard to explore ships and shipping further.

Many cruise companies have a complex history. From the heady early days of cruising, two world wars, the depression, a rise in car ownership and cheap foreign holidays, the fortunes of cruise companies have mirrored the social and economic history of these islands. Brothers, cousins, adventurers and even a well born scoundrel (or two), can all lay claim to their place in the history of cruise shipping on the Mersey as companies broke up, reformed and combined throughout the years.

In Anglo-Saxon times, the Mersey is said to have been the border between Northumbria and Mercia and for centuries it formed part of the boundary between the historic counties of Lancashire and Cheshire. Its name probably originated from the Old English Maeres-ea, meaning border river. However today it flows through the metropolitan county of Merseyside

The River Mersey has always been essential to the life and trade of Liverpool and the north-west of England, but until the mid-1800s ships visiting the port were mainly concerned with moving cargo. Salt from Cheshire, coal from Lancashire, pottery from Staffordshire, metal from Birmingham and sheep from Wales were all transported out of the country on ships from the Mersey Docks. The world's first enclosed wet dock was built in Liverpool in 1715 and in 1847, the first floating landing stage opened at Liverpool. The landing stage rose and fell with tide so that the ships could berth at any time. For construction of the quays the Mersey Docks and Harbour Board used granite from a quarry it owned in Kirkmabreck, Scotland. Seaforth Dock, a Freeport on the Liverpool side of the estuary where it meets Liverpool Bay, opened in 1971.

The River Mersey is 70 miles (112 km) long, and is formed when three tributaries – the River Goyt, the River Tame and the River Etherow – merge in Stockport. Between high and low tide, the river can rise and fall by around 30ft. This is the second highest rise in the British Isles, after the River Severn. The estuary narrows between Liverpool and Birkenhead, where it is constricted to a width of 0.7 miles (1.1 km), between Albert Dock in Liverpool and the Woodside ferry terminal in Birkenhead. The original course of the river has been obliterated by the Manchester Ship Canal past Hollins Green to Rixton, but the old river bed can be seen outside Irlam and at Warburton.

There are three tunnels under the Mersey; the oldest is the rail tunnel which was opened in 1886, and two road tunnels, the Queensway Tunnel, opened in 1934, connects the city to Birkenhead, and the Kingsway Tunnel, opened in 1971, which connects with Wallasey. The Silver Jubilee

Bridge completed in 1961, crosses between Runcorn and Widnes and there is a railway bridge adjacent to the Silver Jubilee Bridge.

It is said that rowing across the Mersey takes 90 minutes in calm weather so it is not at all surprising that a ferry across the Mersey from Seacombe, the narrowest crossing point of the river, is recorded in the Doomsday Book of 1086. Today the Mersey ferry operates between Pier Head in Liverpool and Woodside in Birkenhead and Seacombe. It has become a tourist attraction offering cruises that provide an overview of the river and surrounding areas.

In the arts the river has given its name to the 'Merseybeat', sound, developed by bands from Liverpool, notably the Beatles, and in 1965 the Mersey was the subject of a top-ten hit single "Ferry Cross the Mersey" by Gerry and the Pacemakers. The Liverpool poets Roger McGough, Brian Patten and Adrian Henri published an anthology of their work, The Mersey Sound, in 1967. The Mersey is also considered sacred by British Hindus, and worshipped in a similar way to the River Ganges. Festival of Immersion ceremonies are held annually on the river, in which clay figures representing the Hindu Lord Ganesha, the elephant deity riding a mouse, are submerged in the river from a ferry boat. Followers throw flowers, pictures and coins into the river.

Most of the conurbation on both sides of the estuary is known as Merseyside and it is obvious that the influence of the river on the life of those who live and work there is immense. Cruise ships and their passengers complete the circle of social and economic history that is said to have started in 1835 when a sailor called Arthur Anderson from the Shetland Isles wrote about his vision of providing passenger services from Scotland to Iceland, Spain and Portugal. Two years later he co-founded the Peninsular and Oriental Steam Navigation Company (P&O), and passenger cruising was born.

Ian Collard, Merseyside. April 2016.

Accra 1947

11,644 grt. 143.6 x 20.2m built Vickers Armstrong, Barrow. Yard No 948.

Anslem 1950

10,990 grt. 153.7 x 19.6 x 10.36m 15½ knots. b. John Cockerill S.A., Hoboken. Yard No 720.

In the 1960s and 1970s many shipping companies encouraged passengers to cruise on their vessels while they were on a regular liner service.

Elder Dempster Lines operated a passenger and cargo service from Liverpool to West Africa by *Aureol*, *Accra* and *Apapa*.

The vessels loaded cargo at Brocklebank Dock and moved to Princes Landing Stage to allow the passengers to board.

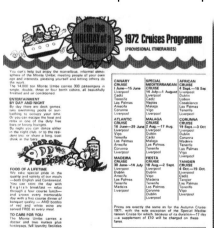

Anselm was built as *Baudouinville* for Cie Maritime Belge, Antwerp, for their service from Antwerp to Matadi. She was renamed *Thysville* in 1957 and was purchased by the Booth Line 1961, becoming *Anselm*.

She was transferred to the Blue Star Line two years later and renamed *Iberia Star*. In 1965 she was transferred to Austasia Limited, becoming *Australasia* for the Singapore to Melbourne service.

She was purchased by Euroasia Carriers Limited, Singapore in 1972, and broken up at Kaohsiung the following year.

Arkadia
1931
22,424 grt.
176.48 x 23.38 x 11.89m.
20 knots.
b. Vickers Armstrong Limited, Newcastle.
Yard No 1.

Arkadia is seen here in the Mersey off Birkenhead. *Arkadia* was built as ***Monarch of Bermuda*** and was owned by Furness Withy to operate on the New York to Hamilton, Bermuda service with her sister, the ***Queen of Bermuda***. In 1939 she became a troop carrier and operated to Norway, Europe and North Africa. At the end of the war she had transported 164,840 personnel and steamed 450,512 miles.

She was purchased by the Ministry of Transport, and after her rebuild by J.I. Thornycroft, she was renamed ***New Australia*** and employed as an emigrant carrier. She sailed on her first voyage from Southampton to Sydney on 15 August 1950, managed by Shaw, Savill & Albion.

In 1953 she carried troops to Korea and, in 1958 was sold to the Greek Line and was renamed ***Arkadia***. She was broken up in Valencia during December 1966.

Carinthia

1925   20,277 grt. 183.06 x 22.45 x 12.34m. 330 first,
420 second, 1,500 third class passengers.   16½ knots.
b. Vickers Armstrong & Company Limited, Barrow. Yard No 586.

Carinthia was built as a sister to *Franconia* (2) and was laid down as *Servia* by Vickers Armstrong & Company at Barrow. She was launched as *Carinthia* on 24 February 1925, and operated on the Liverpool - New York route during the winter months. In 1930 she was also chartered by Furness Withy for their New York - Bermuda service. On 3 September, 1939, the day Britain declared war on Germany she left New York for Liverpool and later that year she was converted to an Armed Merchant Cruiser. On 6 June 1940 she was torpedoed by *U-46*, west of Ireland but remained afloat for 35 hours while all on board were rescued. Sadly, four of her crew lost their lives in the initial explosion.

Empress of Britain

1956   25,516 grt.   195.08 x 25.96 x 14.63m.   160 first, 894 tourist class passengers.
b. Fairfield Shipbuilding & Engineering Company Limited, Govan.
IMO 5103924.

Empress of Britain was launched by H M Queen Elizabeth on 22 June 1955 and sailed on her maiden voyage from Liverpool to Quebec and Montreal on 20 April 1956. Following completion of voyage 123 for her owners she was chartered to the Travel Savings Association in 1963, cruising from Cape Town to South America. She was returned to Canadian Pacific the following year and sold to the Greek Line, becoming *Queen Anna Maria*. Following a refit at Genoa she operated on the Piraeus - Naples - New York service, later sailing from Haifa to New York. Early in 1975 she was laid up at Piraeus and sold to Carnival Cruise Lines, becoming *Carnivale* and cruised out of Miami. She became *Olympic* in 1993, *The Topaz* in 1998 and was broken up in 2008.

Franconia

1923
20,175 grt.
190.5 x 22.45 x 12.34m.
330 first, 420 second,
1,500 third class
passengers.
16½ knots.
b. John Brown &
Company Limited,
Clydebank.
Yard No 492.

Franconia was built for the Cunard Line, to operate on the Liverpool - New York route and cruising in the winter months. In 1926 she went aground at San Juan, Puerto Rico, and in 1931 was chartered to Furness Withy for their New York-Bermuda service.

Franconia operated on the London - New York route in 1934 and from Liverpool the following year. In 1938 she undertook a world cruise which included 37 ports and 41,727 miles. The following year she was requisitioned as a troopship and assisted in evacuating troops from Norway and France in 1940. During the Second World War she also operated to the Middle East, the Mediterranean and Cape Town, via the Suez Canal. In 1945 she hosted the Crimean Yalta Conference between Churchill, Roosevelt and Stalin, and was involved in troop repatriation duties the year after.

In 1949 she was returned to her owners and placed on the Liverpool to Canada route, and ran aground again off Quebec in 1950. Following engine problems in 1954 she was forced to return to Southampton and repairs took two months to complete. Following a season of cruising from New York in 1956 she was sold to Thos W Ward and broken up at Inverkeithing.

Hibernian Coast
1946   1,258 grt.   79.24 x 12.19 x 4.72m.   14 knots.
b. Hall Russell & Company Ltd, Aberdeen.
Yard No 800.

Hilary
1931 7,403 grt.   129.3 x 17.13m. 14 knots.
b. Cammell, Laird and Co., Birkenhead.
Yard No 975.

Hibernian Coast offered cruises from Liverpool to Dublin, Cork, Plymouth, Southampton and London. Single and double cabins were available with a lounge, dining room and bar provided.

She was named *Aberdonian Coast* by her first owners, the Aberdeen Steam Navigation Company. Then she was renamed *Hibernian Coast* by Coast Lines in 1948. Then following sale to Alomar Mechanical Engineering Co. Kuwait, renamed *Port Said Coast* in 1968. She was broken up at Mercia, Spain in 1974.

Hilary was built in 1931 by Cammell Laird & Company Limited at Birkenhead for Booth Line's Liverpool - Manaus service.

In 1940 she became HMS *Hilary* and operated in the North Atlantic. In 1943 she became an Infantry Landing Ship and was used as the headquarters ship for the invasion of Sicily, and later for the invasion of Salerno.

On 6 June 1944 she was the headquarters for the invasion of Normandy and was eventually decommissioned the following year at the end of the war.

She returned to commercial service later in 1945 and following a refit in 1956 was chartered to Elder Dempster Line for their West Africa services.

After her final sailing to South America in 1959 she was sold to Thos W Ward to be broken up at Inverkeithing.

Laconia

1922
19,695 grt.
183.29 x 22.48 x 12.4m.
350 first, 350 second,
1,500 third class
passengers,
16 knots.
b. Swan Hunter &
Wigham Richardson
Limited, Wallsend on
Tyne.
Yard No 1125.

Laconia initially operated on the Southampton - New York route and later from Liverpool. In 1923 she made a number of sailings from Hamburg to New York and in the 1930s she carried out cruises from British ports and New York. In 1939 she became an Armed Merchant Cruiser and a troopship two years later.

On 12 September 1942 she was torpedoed by **U-156** with 2,200 passengers on board, which included 1,800 Italian prisoners of war. It was the first time in the war that a U-boat commander sent a message appealing for help and stated that he would not retaliate. The French sent vessels with **U-506** and **U-507** assisting in ferrying passengers to the French warships.

On 16 September an American Liberator bombed **U-156**, while she was towing lifeboats. The following day **U-506** was also bombed with 142 survivors on her decks. Following the incident Adolf Hitler issued an order that U-boats should not attempt to assist survivors in the future.

Lady Killarney

1912   2,284 grt. 99.18 x 12.71 x 4.93m.   18 knots.
b. Harland & Wolff Limited, Belfast. Yard No 424.

Lady Killarney was built as the ***Patriotic*** for the Belfast Steamship Company. She was acquired by Coast Lines Ltd, in 1919 and transferred to the British & Irish Steam Packet Company Ltd in 1930, becoming ***Lady Leinster***. In 1938 she was renamed ***Lady Connaught*** and was badly damaged by a mine in 1940 on a voyage from Liverpool to Belfast.

During the Second World War she operated as a cattle carrier and hospital ship. In 1946 she was converted to a cruise ship, managed by Coast Lines and renamed ***Lady Killarney***. She was broken up at Port Glasgow in 1956.

11

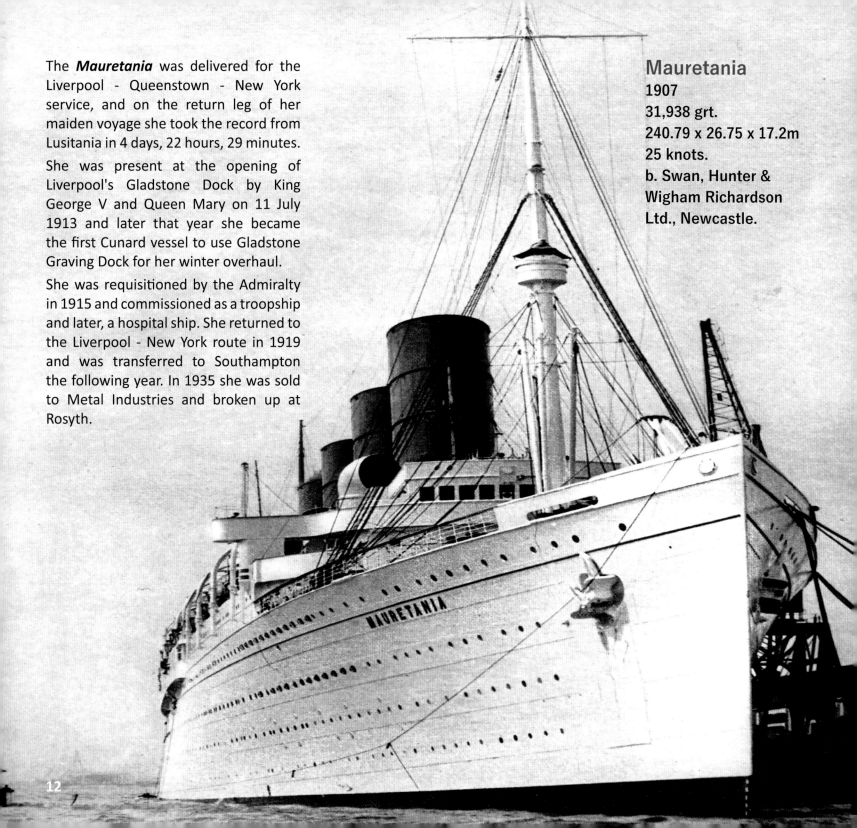

The *Mauretania* was delivered for the Liverpool - Queenstown - New York service, and on the return leg of her maiden voyage she took the record from Lusitania in 4 days, 22 hours, 29 minutes.

She was present at the opening of Liverpool's Gladstone Dock by King George V and Queen Mary on 11 July 1913 and later that year she became the first Cunard vessel to use Gladstone Graving Dock for her winter overhaul.

She was requisitioned by the Admiralty in 1915 and commissioned as a troopship and later, a hospital ship. She returned to the Liverpool - New York route in 1919 and was transferred to Southampton the following year. In 1935 she was sold to Metal Industries and broken up at Rosyth.

Mauretania
1907
31,938 grt.
240.79 x 26.75 x 17.2m
25 knots.
b. Swan, Hunter & Wigham Richardson Ltd., Newcastle.

Monte Anaga   1959
6,813 grt.   130.8x18.1m.
b. Euskalduna, Olaveaga, Bilbao.   Yard No 137.

Queen of Bermuda   1933
22,575 grt. 176.48 x 23.38 x 11.89m. 20 knots
b. Vickers Armstrong Ltd. Newcastle.   Yard No 681.

The Spanish Aznar Line inaugurated passenger and cargo services from London to the Canary Islands in 1952 and from Liverpool in 1959. One class cruises were offered to Portugal, Vigo, Madeira and Las Palmas/Santa Cruz.

Monte Anaga was sold to the Government of Mexico in 1975 and renamed **Primero De Junio**. She was deleted from registers in 2002.

Queen of Bermuda was built for Furness, Withy & Company's service from New York to Hamilton, Bermuda.

In 1939 she was converted to an Armed Merchant Cruiser and fitted with guns and anti-aircraft weapons. Her third funnel was removed and she saw service in the South Atlantic and became a troop ship in 1943.

Queen of Bermuda was refitted in 1947, her third funnel replaced, and her original eight boilers were replaced by three.

She returned to the New York - Bermuda service on 12 February 1949, and in her 1961/62 winter overhaul, she was rebuilt with one funnel. She continued in service until 1966, when she was broken up at Faslane.

SUN, SEA AND THE CANARIES
WITH THE AZNAR LINE
VIGO–LAS PALMAS–TENERIFFE

Reina Del Pacifico
1931
17,702 grt.
168.05 x 23.27 x 11.51m.
280 first, 162 second,
446 third class
passengers.
18 knots.
b. Harland & Wolff
Limited, Belfast.
Yard No 852.

Reina Del Pacifico was delivered on 23 September 1930 for the Pacific Steam Navigation Company's service from Liverpool to South America. She sailed on her maiden voyage on 9 April 1931 to La Rochelle, Vigo, Bermuda, Bahamas, Havana, Jamaica, Panama Canal, Guayaquil, Callao and Antofagasta, a voyage of 25½ days.

On 19 January 1932 she left Liverpool to recommence the 'Round South America' cruise, which she undertook once a year.

She was requisitioned by the Admiralty and left the Clyde in a convoy of 17 ships for the Far East on 7 September 1939. *Reina Del Pacifico* was converted to a troopship later that year and saw service in Norway, West Africa and Cape Town in 1940. Following a distinguished war service she was returned to her builders where 28 people lost their lives in an engine room explosion on 11 September 1947. She returned to the South American service the following year.

On 8 July 1957 she went aground at Bermuda and was refloated two days later but lost a propeller at Havana later that year. She left Liverpool on 27 April 1958 for her last voyage to South American ports and on her return she was sold to John Cashmore and broken up at Newport, Wales.

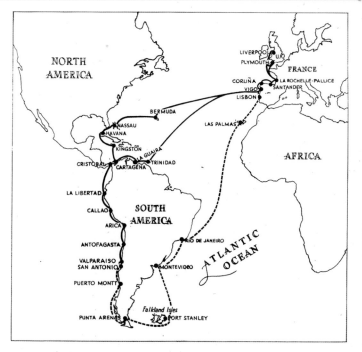

THE SERVICES

PASSENGER SERVICE. Liverpool to West Coast, via France, Spain, Bermuda, Bahamas, Cuba, Jamaica, Trinidad, Venezuela, Colombia and the Panama Canal.

EXPRESS CARGO-PASSENGER SERVICE. United Kingdom and Continental ports to the West Coast, direct via the Panama Canal.

ISLAND CARGO-PASSENGER SERVICE. United Kingdom ports to Bermuda, Bahamas and Cuba.

ROUND SOUTH AMERICA. Occasional voyages by the passenger ships, completing the circuit, via Puerto Monte, Punta Arenas, Port Stanley, Montevideo, Rio de Janeiro and Las Palmas.

THE FLEET

	GR. TONS	YEAR BUILT
Albemarle	3,364	1950
Cotopaxi	8,559	1953
Cuzco	8,038	1951
Flamenco	8,491	1950
Kenuta	8,494	1950
Pizarro	8,564	1955
Potosi	8,564	1955
Reina del Mar	20,225	1956
Reina del Pacifico	17,872	1931
Salamanca	6,704	1948
Salaverry	6,647	1946
Salinas	6,705	1947
Samanco	6,413	1943
Santander	6,648	1946
Sarmiento	6,393	1943
Walsingham	3,343	1950

Pacific Steam Navigation Company - founded 1838

In 1852 the company gained a contract for British Government mail to posts in western South America. Two direct routes were also established - Liverpool to Callao in 1868 and London to Sydney in 1877. In 1910 the Royal Mail Steam Packet Company bought the entire company but the name and routes were retained until Furness Withy bought Royal Mail in 1965. Following the purchase the separate Pacific Steam Navigation Company structure was abolished and the vessels rebranded, effectively signalling the end of the company.

Royal Iris
1951   1,234 grt.   48.46 x 14.63 x 2.74m.   1,000 passengers   12 knots.
b. Wm Denny & Brothers Limited, Dumbarton.   Yard No 1448.

Royal Iris is seen here berthing at Liverpool Landing Stage on a cruise from New Brighton. In 1994 she was sold as a restaurant ship berthed at Liverpool Landing Stage. She was moved to Cardiff in 1995 and to London in 1998. In 2015 she is berthed on the Thames at Greenwich.

DON'T MISS THE BOAT

GREAT SUMMER SAIL

Royal Iris service cruises 1971

DATE 1971	DEPARTS NEW BRIGHTON	DEPARTS SEACOMBE	DEPARTS LIVERPOOL	RETURNS NEW BRIGHTON	RETURNS SEACOMBE	RETURNS L'POOL
JULY						
Thursday 1st			16.35		17.15	17.35
Saturday 3rd		15.15	15.35		17.15	17.35
Sunday 4th		15.15	15.35		17.15	17.35
Tuesday 6th	15.15		15.35		17.15	17.35
Wednesday 7th	15.15		15.35	17.15		17.35
Thursday 8th	15.15		16.35	17.15		17.35
Saturday 10th	15.15		16.35	17.15		17.35
Sunday 11th	15.15		15.35	17.15		17.35
Tuesday 13th	15.15		15.35	17.15		17.35
Wednesday 14th	15.15		15.35	17.15		17.35
Sunday 15th		16.15	15.35		17.15	17.35
Thursday 17th		16.15	15.35		17.15	17.35
Saturday 17th		16.15	15.35		17.15	17.35
Sunday 20th		16.15	15.35		17.15	17.35
Tuesday 21st	15.15		16.35	17.15		17.35
Wednesday 22nd	15.15		15.35		17.15	17.35
Thursday 24th	15.15		15.35	17.15		17.35
Saturday 25th	15.15		15.35	17.15		17.35
Sunday 27th	15.15		15.35	17.15		17.35
Tuesday 28th	15.15		15.35			17.35
Wednesday 29th	15.15					
Thursday 31st	15.15			17.15	17.15	17.35
AUGUST						
Sunday 1st	15.15		15.35		17.15	17.35
Tuesday 3rd		15.15	15.35		17.15	17.35
Wednesday 4th		15.15	15.35		17.15	17.35
Thursday 5th		15.15	15.35		17.15	17.35
Friday 6th			15.35	17.15		17.35
Saturday 7th	15.15		15.35	17.15		17.35
Sunday 8th	15.15		15.35	17.15		17.35
Tuesday 10th	15.15		16.35	17.15		17.35
Wednesday 11th	15.15		15.35	17.15		17.35
Thursday 12th	15.15		15.35	17.15		17.35
Saturday 14th	15.15		15.35	17.15		17.35
Sunday 15th	15.15		16.35		17.15	17.35
Tuesday 17th	15.15	15.15	15.35		17.15	17.35
Wednesday 18th		15.15	15.35	17.15		17.35
Thursday 19th		15.15	15.35	17.15		17.35
Saturday 21st		15.15	15.35	17.15		17.35
Sunday 22nd	15.15		15.35	17.15		17.35
Tuesday 24th	15.15		15.35	17.15		17.35
Wednesday 25th	15.15		15.35	17.15		17.35
Thursday 26th	15.15		15.35	17.15		17.35
Saturday 28th	15.15		15.35			
Sunday 29th	15.15			17.15	17.15	17.35
Monday 30th	15.15		15.35	17.15	17.15	17.35
SEPTEMBER						
Saturday 4th	15.15		15.35	17.15	17.15	17.35
Sunday 5th	15.15		15.35			
Sunday 12th	15.15		15.35			
Sunday 19th	15.15		15.35			
Sunday 26th	15.15		15.35			

PRICES	Adults	Children
TUESDAYS TO FRIDAYS	25p	12½p
SATURDAYS, SUNDAYS & BANK HOLIDAYS	35p	17½p

MERSEYSIDE PASSENGER TRANSPORT EXECUTIVE
Telephone No: 051-639 6021.

New Brighton's Unrivalled attraction!

SEA and RIVER CRUISES on Luxurious Ferry Steamers

DANCE CRUISES WITH FIRST CLASS
DANCE BANDS, LICENSED BARS
:: AND RUNNING BUFFETS ::
PARTIES BOOKED IN ADVANCE

REGULAR FERRY SERVICE TO AND FROM LIVERPOOL

For further details apply:—
Ferries General Manager,
Seacombe. Ferry, Wallasey.
Tel. Wallasey 3671/2.

ROYAL IRIS CRUISES 1971

Hundreds of thousands of families from all parts of Britain have enjoyed a cruise on the Royal Iris... one of the world's most famous pleasure cruise ships.

This unique vessel sails from Liverpool, New Brighton (when tides permit) and Seacombe from Easter onwards.

There are good sun decks where you and the family can relax when the weather is fine. When it is not so sunny you can sit in the air-conditioned saloons and enjoy the passing panorama of the Mersey scene through wide windows.

The captain, incidentally, gives a commentary on the shipping and shore activities.

For the young ... and not-so-young ... there is music for dancing in the ballroom which has a maple sprung floor. Refreshment buffets ensure that you can assuage any appetite developed by the invigorating river breezes. And, of course, the famous fish and chip restaurant will be a sure attraction for the youngsters.

FULLY LICENSED BARS ARE OPEN AT ALL TIMES DURING CRUISING.

The two-hour cruises begin at New Brighton or nearby Seacombe at 3.15 p.m. calling at Liverpool 20 minutes later and return to New Brighton or Seacombe at 5.15 p.m. to finish at Liverpool at 5.35 p.m... just in time to get home conveniently for tea or dinner. Buses run right to the Pier Head at Liverpool and New Brighton landing stages. Alternatively there is ample car parking space at Seacombe and the Pier Head.

Educational Cruises

Inquire at the MPTE Ferries Dept., Seaview Road, Wallasey (051-639 6021) for the separate brochure describing the special cruises for school-children aboard the Royal Daffodil.

This may be the last year when the Royal Iris or the service ferry boats can use the New Brighton landing stage because of siltation. So why not make sure that you and your children can enjoy this river approach to the Mersey's well-known holiday resort this week-end.

Why Not Have a Party?

Hundreds of party organisers from as far away as Lancaster or Bristol book the Royal Iris for dances or social evenings. Ask NOW for details. Charter rates vary between £80 and £100 for a three-hour cruise. Capacity is 600.

Birkenhead and Wallasey followed different themes in naming their ferries; Birkenhead used local place names such as Woodchurch and Claughton, and Wallasey used flowers, such as Daffodil, Primrose and Iris.

17

Southern Cross

1955
20,204 grt.
184.1 x 23.77 x 13.81m.
1,160 passengers (one class).
20 knots.
b. Harland & Wolff Limited, Belfast.
Yard No 1498.

Southern Cross and her sister **Northern Star** were built for the Shaw, Savill Line's round the world service. The **Southern Cross** sailed on her maiden voyage from Southampton on 29 March 1955.

In 1971 she completed a series of cruises from Liverpool and was laid up at Southampton later that year. She was sold in 1973, renamed **Calypso** and refitted at Piraeus as a cruise ship. She became **Azure Seas** in 1980, **Ocean Breeze** in 1991 and was broken up at Chittagong in 2003.

Shaw, Savill & Albion Line – shortened to Shaw, Savill Line in marketing materials, was made up of three different companies; Shaw, Savill & Co, formed in 1858, Albion Line formed in Glasgow in 1856 and John Leslie & Partners of Aberdeen. The combined company was created in 1882 but Shaw, Savill & Co retained five sailing ships. Shaw, Savill & Albion Line also ran a joint service to New Zealand with White Star Line from 1884 to 1933. Control of Shaw, Savill was acquired by Furness, Withy & Co. in 1933.

St Tudno   1926

2,326 grt   102 x 14 x 6m.   19 knots   b. Fairfield Shipbuilding and Engineering Company Limited, Govan.   Yard No 618.

St Tudno operated cruises from Liverpool to Llandudno and Menai Bridge. She was broken up at Ghent in 1963.

The New North Wales Steam Ship Company was a pleasure cruise company formed in Liverpool in 1890. So great was their successful first season that only a year later they took over the rival Liverpool Llandudno and Welsh Coast Steam Boat Company to form the Liverpool and North Wales Steam Ship Company (LNWSC). At the start of the 1950s the LNWSC suffered from the excursion market's decline due to competition from buses and later, privately owned cars. The company went into voluntary liquidation at the end of the 1962 season.

Sylvania
1957
22,017 grt.
185.4 x 29.49 x 14.1m.
125 first, 800 tourist class passengers (one class when cruising)
20 knots.
b. John Brown & Company Limited, Clydebank.
Yard No 700.

From 1925 onwards "Short sea passages and cruises by Great Floating Hotels" were advertised by the Cunard Line as "a desirable means of crossing the Irish Sea" by *Caronia*, *Carmania Franconia*, *Laconia*, *Scythia*, *Samaria* and *Aurania*. These short cruises continued to be offered by the shipping line after the Second World War by the motorships *Britannic* and *Sylvania* in the 1960s.

In 1879 the privately held British and North American Royal Mail Steam Packet Company was reorganised as a public stock corporation, the Cunard Steamship Company, Ltd. Cunard was an innovative and award winning and record breaking shipping company in an age of fierce competition and rivalry.

In 1916 Cunard Line completed its European headquarters in Liverpool, moving in on 12 June of that year. The grand neo-Classical Cunard Building was the third of Liverpool's 'Three Graces'. The headquarters were used by Cunard until the 1960s.

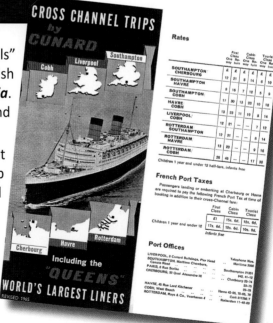

21

Uganda

1952
14,430 grt.
164.53 x 21.73 x
10.67m.
18 knots.
b. Barclay, Curle &
Company, Scotstoun.
Yard No 720.

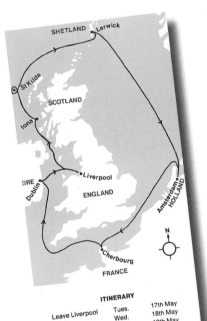

ITINERARY

Leave Liverpool	Tues.	17th May
Iona	Wed.	18th May
St. Kilda	Thurs.	19th May
Lerwick	Fri.	20th May
Amsterdam	Sun./Mon.	22/23rd May
Cherbourg	Wed.	25th May
Dublin	Fri./Sat.	27/28th May
Return Liverpool	Sun.	29th May

The British India Line ship *Uganda* was built for service between London and East Africa. She sailed on her maiden voyage from London to Beira on 2 August 1951. The East African service was withdrawn in 1966 and it was decided to convert her to an educational cruise ship at Hamburg in 1967. She sailed on her first cruise on 27 February the following year.

In 1972 her ownership was transferred to the P&O Line. On 10 April 1982 she was requisitioned by the British Government and operated as a hospital ship in the Falkland Islands. She resumed cruises briefly later that year, but was chartered to the government again in 1983 for use between the Ascension Islands and the Falklands. She returned to the United Kingdom in 1985, and the following year she was laid up and sold to ship-breakers at Kaohsiung. *Uganda* was renamed *Triton* for her last voyage. On arrival she was anchored outside the harbour while negotiations took place for a possible re-sale. However on 22 August 1986 she was driven aground by typhoon Wayne and heeled over onto her side, being demolished as she lay.

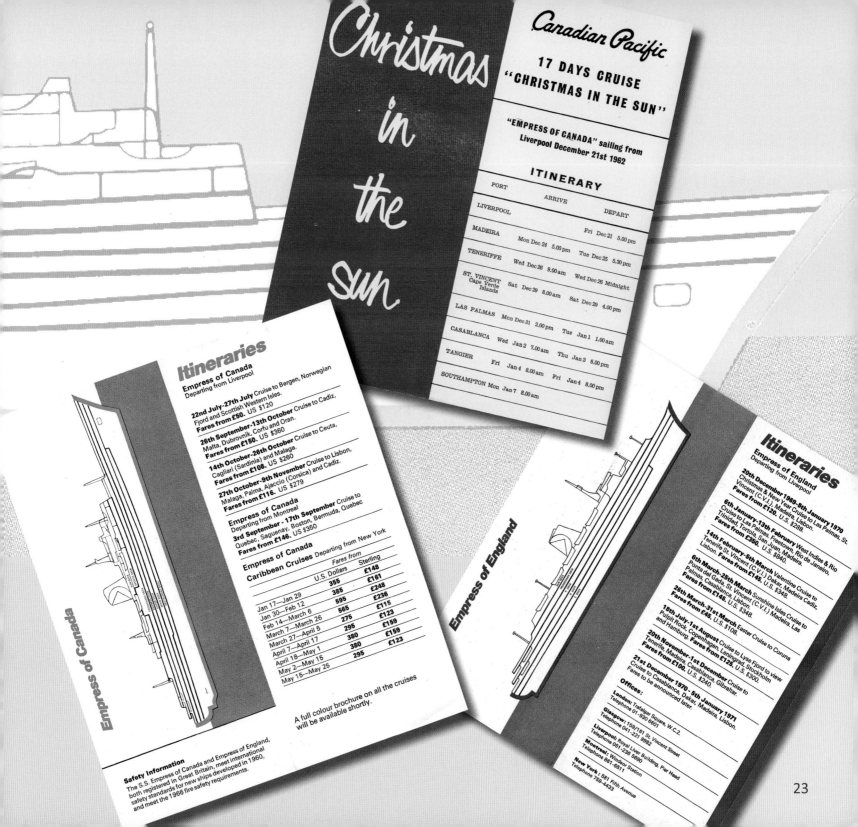

Christmas in the sun

17 DAYS CRUISE "CHRISTMAS IN THE SUN"

"EMPRESS OF CANADA" sailing from
Liverpool December 21st 1962

ITINERARY

PORT	ARRIVE	DEPART
LIVERPOOL		Fri Dec 21 5.00 pm
MADEIRA	Mon Dec 24 5.00 pm	Tue Dec 25 5.30 pm
TENERIFFE	Wed Dec 26 9.00 am	Wed Dec 26 Midnight
ST. VINCENT Cape Verde Islands	Sat Dec 29 8.00 am	Sat Dec 29 4.00 pm
LAS PALMAS	Mon Dec 31 2.00 pm	Tue Jan 1 1.00 am
CASABLANCA	Wed Jan 2 7.00 am	Thu Jan 3 8.00 pm
TANGIER	Fri Jan 4 8.00 am	Fri Jan 4 8.00 pm
SOUTHAMPTON	Mon Jan 7 8.00 am	

Itineraries

Empress of Canada
Departing from Liverpool

22nd July-27th July Cruise to Bergen, Norwegian Fjord and Scottish Western Isles. **Fares from £50.** US $120

26th September-13th October Cruise to Cadiz, Malta, Dubrovnik, Corfu and Oran. **Fares from £150.** US $360

14th October-26th October Cruise to Ceuta, Cagliari (Sardinia) and Malaga. **Fares from £108.** US $260

27th October-9th November Cruise to Lisbon, Malaga, Palma, Ajaccio (Corsica) and Cadiz. **Fares from £116.** US $279

Empress of Canada
Departing from Montreal

3rd September - 17th September Cruise to Quebec, Saguenay, Boston, Bermuda, Quebec. **Fares from £146.** US $350

Empress of Canada
Caribbean Cruises Departing from New York

	Fares from	
	U.S. Dollars	Sterling
	355	£148
Jan 17—Jan 29		£161
Jan 30—Feb 12	385	£248
Feb 14—March 6	595	£236
March 7—March 26	565	£115
March 27—April 5	275	£123
April 7—April 17	295	£159
April 18—May 1	380	£159
May 2—May 15	380	£123
May 15—May 25	295	

A full colour brochure on all the cruises
will be available shortly.

Empress of Canada

Safety Information
The S.S. Empress of Canada and Empress of England, both registered in Great Britain, meet international safety standards for new ships developed in 1960, and meet the 1966 fire safety requirements.

Empress of England

Itineraries

Empress of England
Departing from Liverpool

20th December 1969-5th January 1970 Christmas & New Year Cruise to Las Palmas, St. Vincent (C.V.I.) Madeira, Lisbon. **Fares from £120.** U.S. $288.

6th January-13th February West Indies & Rio Cruise to Las Palmas, Freetown, St. Lucia, Trinidad, Tortola, San Juan, Rio de Janeiro, **Fares from £350.** U.S. $840.

14th February-5th March Valentine Cruise to Teneriffe St. Vincent (C.V.I.) Madeira, Lisbon. **Fares from £145.** U.S. $348.

6th March-25th March Sunshine Isles Cruise to Ponta del Gada, St. Vincent (C.V.I.) Dakar, Madeira Cadiz, Palmas, Casablanca, Lisbon. **Fares from £145.** U.S. $348.

26th March-31st March Easter Cruise to Coruna Teneriffe, Madeira, Lisbon. **Fares from £45.** U.S. $108.

18th July-1st August Cruise to Lyse Fjord to view Pulpit Rock, Copenhagen, Leningrad Stockholm and Hamburg. **Fares from £125.** U.S. $300.

20th November-1st December Cruise to Casablanca, Dakar, Madeira, Gibraltar. **Fares from £100.** U.S. $240.

21st December 1970 - 5th January 1971 Cruise to Casablanca, Madeira, Lisbon. Fares to be announced later.

Offices:

London: Trafalgar Square, W.C.2.
Telephone 01-930 6601.

Glasgow: 159/161 St. Vincent Street.
Telephone 041-221 9982.

Liverpool: Royal Liver Building, Pier Head
Telephone 051-236 5690

Montreal: Windsor Station
Telephone 861-6511

New York: 581 Fifth Avenue
Telephone 759-1433

Vandyck

1921
13,233 grt.
155.63 x 19.6 x 11.98m.
300 first, 150 second,
230 third class
passengers.
14 knots.
b. Workman, Clark &
Company Limited,
Belfast.
Yard No 359.

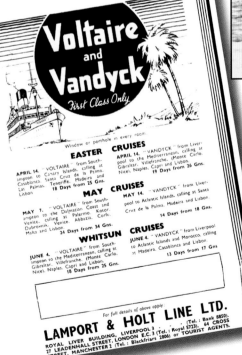

Vandyck was built in Belfast in 1921 for Lamport & Holt's Liverpool to Brazil and River Plate service but her delivery was delayed because of vibration problems. She was designed to carry enough oil for the round voyage.

In 1922 she made one voyage from New York to Hamburg for the Royal Mail Line. She was laid up at Southampton in 1930 and converted to a cruise vessel two years later. In 1939 she was also requisitioned by the Admiralty and converted to an Armed Boarding vessel, becoming HMS *Vandyck*. Following a voyage to Canada she was sent to Scapa Flow as an accommodation ship and later a depot ship to the patrol vessels. In 1940 she participated in the Norway campaign and was damaged by the *Admiral Hipper*. *Vandyck* was attacked by German aircraft on 9 June and set on fire off Harstad, near Narvik. The following day she was abandoned, and her crew captured, becoming prisoners of war at Marflag. She finally sank on 11 June.

Voltaire

1923
13,248 grt.
155.63 x 19.6 x 11.98m.
300 first, 150 second,
230 third class
passengers.
14 knots.
b. Workman, Clark &
Company Limited,
Belfast.
Yard No 360.

Voltaire was initially based at New York. Following a period of lay up in the River Blackwater, Essex, she was converted to a cruise ship in 1932. She was requisitioned by the Admiralty in 1939 as a troopship and painted grey at Southampton, then used as an accommodation ship to HMS *Royal Oak* and HMS *Iron Duke* at Scapa Flow.

When *Royal Oak* was torpedoed by *U-47* on 14 October 1939, the survivors were taken on board *Voltaire*. *Iron Duke* was attacked and beached the following day and Voltaire was temporarily named *Iron Duke II*. She was later converted to an Armed Merchant Cruiser on the Tyne, becoming HMS *Voltaire*. In 1940 she was employed as a contraband and inspection vessel between Malta and Alexandria, and then became a North Atlantic escort vessel. In March 1941 she left Halifax for Trinidad and Freetown, and sank on 4 April, following an attack by the German auxiliary cruiser *Thor*. Seventy five of her crew were lost, and 197 survivors were taken on board *Thor*.

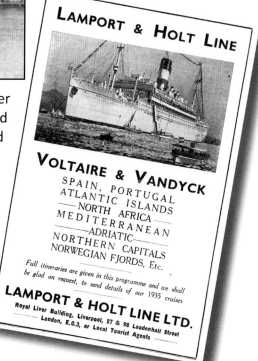

The new Liverpool Cruise Terminal was officially opened by HRH The Duke of Kent on 21 September 2007 with the *Queen Elizabeth 2* berthed at the stage. It is 350 metres (1,150 feet) long and is situated on the Mersey at the Pier Head. This new location enables vessels to visit Liverpool without having to enter the port's dock system. Previously cruise ships had berthed at temporary facilities at Alexandra and Langton Docks or were tendered by the Mersey ferries when anchored in the river.

The project was funded by £9.2 million from the United Kingdom and £8.6 million from the European Union Structural Fund. However the grants were given on the understanding that the terminal would only be used as a port of call and cruises would not be allowed to begin or end at the facility. This clause was included to minimise unfair competition from other ports that had financed their terminals with private funding.

Soon after the terminal was opened it became clear that this clause was restricting the amount of cruises that companies such as Fred. Olsen and Thomson wished to offer from the port and Liverpool City Council tried unsuccessfully in 2009 to have the restriction removed. Following a high profile campaign, the European Commission found that the funding was in line with EU state aid rules.

In 2012 Liverpool City Council agreed to pay back £8.8 million requested by the Government to enable cruises to start and end in the city. The Mayor of Liverpool, Joe Anderson said, "The cruise terminal is proving to be a huge success with positive feedback from operators and passengers. It provides a boost to our tourism industry, creating and sustaining many jobs. Liverpool has an unrivalled maritime history and we are on the way to restoring our reputation as a leading cruise destination." Following this agreement Cruise and Maritime Voyages' *Ocean Countess* sailed on 29 May 2012, the first to cruise to leave Liverpool Pier Head since 1972.

Liverpool can claim that it is one of the few cities in the world where passengers can arrive near to the centre of the city. It was designated a UNESCO World Heritage Site in 2004, European Capital of Culture in 2008, Best UK Port of Call at Cruise Critic United Kingdom's editors pick awards in 2013 and Seatrade Cruise Awards "Destination of the Year" for 2015. Liverpool Cruise Terminal continues to grow. *Queen Mary 2* arrived at Liverpool on 24 May 2015 and was joined by her fleet mates *Queen Elizabeth* and *Queen Victoria* the following day.

On 4 July *Queen Mary 2* sailed to New York, 175 years to the day when Cunard's *Britannia* departed on her maiden voyage from Liverpool. The Cruise Terminal also welcomed back the *Seven Seas Voyager*, which was the first cruise ship to call at the new facility on 9 September 2007.

Adonia

2001
30,277 gt.
710 passengers.
181 x 25.5 x 5.8m.
18 knots.
b. Chantiers de l'Atlantique, St Nazaire, France.
Yard No X31
IMO 9210220

P&O Cruises

The **Adonia** was built as **R Eight** for Renaissance Cruises, which entered administration in 2001 when the ship was laid up in Gibraltar. She was placed on a seven-year charter to Swan Hellenic in 2002, becoming **Minerva II.** She was acquired by Carnival in 2006 and placed with Princess Cruises as **Royal Princess**, the following year. In 2011 she was transferred to the P&O fleet, and given the name **Adonia**. She was the smallest of P&O's ships, carrying 710 passengers and able to navigate to ports larger vessels are unable to include in their itineraries. In 2015 the Carnival Corporation announced that from 2016 **Adonia** would be reassigned to become the first "fathom" ship, focusing on the growing number of people who want to work alongside local communities as part of their travel experience in areas such as education, the environment and economic development. We see her outward bound in the Mersey.

AIDAblu

2010
71,304 gt.
253.3 x 32.2 x 7.3m.
2,192 passengers.
21 knots.
b. Meyer Werft, Papenburg, Germany.
Yard No 660.
IMO 9398888.

In 1999 P&O and Seetours formed a joint venture, which became Aida Cruises to offer cruises to the German market.

In 2003 when P&O Princess Cruises were merged with the Carnival Corporation the Aida vessels were moved to Costa Cruises and registered in Genoa. Aida Cruises is one of eleven brands operated by the Carnival Corporation, and accounts for 6.5% of its share of revenue and has its own executive team.

AIDAblu was the first of three similar vessels, which were slightly larger than the Aidadiva class.

AIDAcara

1996
38,557 gt.
193.3 x 27.6 x 6.2m.
1,180 passengers.
21 knots.
b. Kvaerner Masa Yards, Turku, Finland.
Yard No 1337.
IMO 9112789.

AIDAcara was built for Deutsch Seetouristik/Arkona Reisen as *Aida* and was sold to the Norwegian Cruise Line in 1997, when the company was experiencing financial difficulties.

She was then chartered back and was repurchased by them two years later, when the company became Aida Cruises.

She was renamed *AIDAcara* in 2001, and has since berthed at the Liverpool Cruise Terminal on several occasions.

Albatros

1957
22,017 gt.
185.4 x 29.49 x 14.1m.
20 knots.
b. John Brown & Company Limited, Clydebank.
Yard No 700.
IMO 5347245

Phoenix Reisen

Albatros was built as *Sylvania* for the Cunard Line's service from Liverpool to Canada. She sailed on her maiden voyage on 5 June 1957 and replaced *Britannic* on the New York route in 1961. In 1965 she made the first cruise for Cunard out of Liverpool since 1939. On 30 November that year she made the last Cunard passenger sailing from Liverpool to New York, and on return was laid up at Southampton.

The following year she was sold to the Fairwind Shipping Corporation, becoming *Fairwind*. In 1972 she was transferred to cruising and was based at Fort Lauderdale. In 1988 she was briefly renamed *Sitmar Fairwind* becoming *Albatros* in 1993.

On 15 May as she was leaving her anchorage off the Isles of Scilly it was discovered that she had collided with the North Bartholomew Rock. A number of fuel tanks had been damaged but there was no pollution. *Albatros* arrived at Southampton on 26 May and repairs were completed on 14 July. She continued to operate as a cruise ship until being sold in 2003. She was given the name *Genoa* for the delivery voyage to the shipbreakers and was beached at Alang on 10 January 2004.

Albatros

1973
28,518 gt.
205.5 x 25.2 x 7.5m
850 passengers.
18½ knots.
b. Wärtsilä, Helsinki,
Finland.
Yard No 397.
IMO 7304314

Phoenix Reisen

This **Albatros** was built as **Royal Viking Sea** for the Royal Viking Line. She was lengthened at Bremerhaven in 1983 and the following year the company was taken over by Kloster Cruise (Norwegian Cruise Line) but continued to operate as a separate unit. In 1991 she became **Royal Odyssey** under the Royal Cruise Line and was sold to Actinor and chartered back. In 1997 she was operating for Norwegian Capricorn Line as **Norwegian Star**, offering cruises from Australia.

As **Norwegian Star 1** in 2001 she was employed by Star Cruises in the Far East, followed by a charter to Crown Investments for service in China. In 2002 she was renamed **Crown** to operate in the Mediterranean, owned by Club Cruise and she was chartered by Phoenix Reisen in 2004 to replace the former Cunard vessel **Sylvania**, which was operating for them as **Albatros**. In 2008 Club Cruise entered into administration and **Albatros** is shown as being owned by Phoenix Reisen.

Apollon
1961
27,284 gt.
198.12 x 26.44 x
14.63m.
b. Vickers Armstrong
(Shipbuilders) Limited,
Walker on Tyne.
IMO 5103936

Direct Cruises

Empress of Canada returned to the Mersey as *Apollon* in 1998 to complete a programme of cruises for Direct Line.

She is seen here on an early morning arrival at Langton lock, prior to embarking passengers and sailing on a cruise to the Mediterranean later that day.

Arcadia

2005
84,342 gt.
285.1 x 32.2 x 7.8m.
1,996 passengers.
22 knots.
b. Fincantieri,
Marghera, Venice, Italy.
Yard No 6078.
IMO 9226906

P&O Cruises

Originally ordered as a Holland America Line vessel, she was later intended to be *Queen Victoria* for the Cunard Line. In 2004 it was decided that she would become *Arcadia* for P&O Cruises.

She was named by Dame Kelly Holmes to operate as an adults only vessel.

In 2008 during her refit by Lloydwerft at Bremerhaven she was fitted with 34 additional cabins.

She is seen leaving the Cruise Terminal at 18.00 hours on a Round Britain cruise.

Astor
1987
20,704 gt.
176.3 x 22.6 x 6.1m.
578 passengers.
16½ knots.
b. Howaldtswerke-
Deutsche Werft, Kiel,
Germany.
Yard No 218.
IMO 8506373

Transocean Kreuzfahrten

The German tour company Transocean Tours Touristik was formed in 1954 to operate river and ocean cruises, mainly for German speaking passengers.

In 2007 they entered the British cruise market firstly with **Arielle** and then with **Marco Polo** the following year. When Transocean Tours became insolvent in 2009 Transocean Kreuzfahrten was formed.

She was delivered as **Astor** and sold to the Black Sea Shipping Company of Odessa, becoming **Fedor Dostoevskiy** in June 1988.

She became **Astor** again in 1995 and was purchased by Premicon in 2006. Cruise and Maritime Voyages offered cruises on **Astor** in 2014.

Astra

1965
5,888 gt.
118 x 16.5 x 5.3m.
328 passengers.
16 knots.
b.Brodogradiliste
Uljanik, Pula,
Yugoslavia.
Yard No 248.
IMO 6419057

Caravella Shipping, Ukraine

Seen in Alexandra Dock *Astra* was built as *Istra* and operated on cruises around the Mediterranean and Aegean seas. She was popular with German passengers and was frequently chartered by tour operators such as Seetours, Gastager, Touropa and Intermaris. In 1991 she was renamed *Astra*, when purchased by Caravella Shipping, registered in Ukraine, and *Astra 1* in 1996, when her owners became the Russian Goring Shipping Company. While on a cruise in 1997 she was arrested at Haifa due to the owners suffering financial difficulties and was placed for sale by auction. She was sold to Constellation Cruise Holiday in 1999, when she became *Arion*, operating for Classic International Cruises following a major overhaul and refit costing US$15 million dollars. She came under Arcalia Ship Management in 2000 and in 2013 she became *Porto* when acquired by Portuscale Cruises.

Asuka II
NYK Cruises
1990 50,142 gt. 240.9 x 29.6 x 7.8m. 873 passengers. 21 knots.
b. Mitsubishi Heavy Industries, Nagasaki, Japan. Yard No 2100.   IMO 8806204

Azerbaydzhan

1975
15,410 gt.
156.2 x 21.8 x 5.9m.
21 knots.
b. Wärtsilä, Turku,
Finland.
Yard No 1221.
IMO 7359474

CTC Lines

Azerbaydzhan is berthed at the former Cruise Terminal at Alexandra Dock preparing to sail on a cruise to the Mediterranean. She was built as one of five ships for the Black Sea Shipping Company and chartered to CTC to cruise from United Kingdom ports. She was transferred from the Russian to the Ukrainian flag in 1991, renamed *Arkadiya* in 1996 and *Island Holiday* the following year.

In 1998 she was operating for the New Commodore Cruise Line as *Enchanted Capri*. When the owners went into administration she was employed as a gambling ship, based at Florida and was chartered by Demar in 2003.

She was purchased by them in 2007 and became an offshore accommodation ship anchored off Mexico.

Azores

1948
16,144 gt.
160 x 21 x 7.6m
16½ knots.
b. Götaverken
Shipyard, Gothenburg,
Sweden.
Yard No 611.
IMO 5383304

Portuscale Cruises

Azores was built for the Swedish America Line as *Stockholm* for the Gothenburg - New York service. On a voyage to New York on 5 July 1956 she collided with the Italian liner *Andrea Doria* off the coast of Nantucket, Massachusetts. *Andrea Doria* quickly developed a list, making it impossible to launch half of the lifeboats. However, the vessel remained afloat for over 11 hours and 1,600 passengers were rescued. 46 people lost their lives.

Stockholm was sold in 1960, becoming *Volkerfreundschaft* to operate for the East German Free Trades Union organisation. In 1985 she was sold again, renamed *Volker*, becoming *Fridtjof Nansen* in 1986. Following a brief period as a refugee ship in Oslo she was purchased by Star Lauro in 1989. She was laid up at Genoa and renamed *Italia 1* and *Italia Prima* in 1993, *Caribe* in 2003, *Athena* in 2005 and the *Azores* in 2013. In January 2015 she commenced operating cruises for Cruise and Maritime Voyages.

Balmoral

1988
43,537 gt.
217.9 x 28.2 x 6.8m.
19 knots.
b. Jos. L Meyer,
Papenburg, Germany.
Yard No 616.
IMO 8506294

Fred. Olsen Cruise Lines

She was built as **Crown Odyssey** for the Royal Cruise Line, which was associated with the Kloster Group in 1990. She became **Norwegian Crown** for Norwegian Cruise Line in 1996, being transferred to Orient Lines in 2000, and reverting to **Crown Odyssey**. In 2003 she became **Norwegian Crown** again for the Norwegian Cruise Line and was sold to Fred. Olsen for delivery in late 2007. Following her acquisition by Fred. Olsen she was fitted with a new 30-metre section and was named **Balmoral**.

When cruise ships call at the Cruise Terminal, the Mersey ferries enjoy increased patronage as the ships are best seen from the river. This late afternoon view shows the ferry **Royal Iris of the Mersey** passing **Balmoral**.

Berlin

1980
9,570 gt.
139.3 x 17.5 x 4.8m.
17 knots.
b. Howaldswerke-
Deutsche Werft, Kiel,
Germany.
Yard No 163.
IMO 7904889

Peter Deilmann

Deilmann entered the cruise market with **Berlin**, which was owned by a consortium of investors. He began by chartering coasters in 1968, and entered into the passenger trade in 1973 with a service using the ferry **Nordlicht** between Neustadt, West Germany and Ronne on the Danish island of Bornholm.

He later started a ferry service between Neustadt and Rodby and operated a route between West and East Germany. Deilmann chartered the **Regina Maris** in 1979 and in 1982 **Berlin** was chartered to the Alfred Holt & Company Limited to operate from Singapore to Australia, as **Princess Mahsuri**.

When the charter was terminated two years later she reverted to **Berlin** and she was lengthened by 17 metres at Rendsburg, Germany, in 1986. In 2005 she operated as **Orange Melody** and was renamed **Spirit of Adventure** when acquired by Fred. Olsen later that year. Following service with them she became **FTI Berlin**, and **Berlin** in 2014.

Black Watch

1972
28,613 gt.
804 passengers.
205.5 x 25.2 x 7.5m.
18½ knots.
b. Wärtsilä, Helsinki,
Finland.
Yard No 395.
IMO 7108930

Fred. Olsen Cruise Lines

Inward bound in the Mersey, **Black Watch** was built as the first of three cruise ships for the Royal Viking Line as **Royal Viking Star**. In 1981 she was lengthened at Bremerhaven, and was transferred to Kloster in 1988, becoming **Westward** in 1991.

She was operated by the Royal Cruise Line in 1994 and renamed **Star Odyssey**. In 1996 she was acquired by Fred. Olsen becoming **Black Watch**, and on 15 November, the following year she suffered engine problems outside Marmaris, Turkey, and was sent to Malta for repairs.

Her machinery was replaced in 2005 during a major overhaul by Blohm & Voss at Hamburg.

Black Prince

1966
11,209 gt.
141.6 x 20 x 6.4m.
18½ knots.
b. Lübecker Flender-
Werke, Lübeck,
Germany.
Yard No 561.
IMO 6613328

Fred. Olsen Cruise Lines

Black Prince entered service between Harwich and Kristiansand and Amsterdam, and the Canary Islands in the winter months.

Between 1970 and 1986 she operated jointly with the Bergen Line and was named *Venus* from May - September annually. Following a brief period on a Copenhagen - Gothenburg service she was refitted for the British cruise market.

In 2009 she was sold to Venezuela, renamed *Ola Esmeralda* but was not allowed to operate on environmental grounds. However she was chartered to the United Nations and used as an accommodation ship following a hurricane at Haiti.

She arrived at Santo Domingo in October 2013 and was broken up.

This photograph bears evidence to the fact that huge quantities of scrap are now exported from Liverpool. The tug *Ashgarth* helps the *Black Prince* to swing in the river.

Boudicca

1973
28,551 gt.
755 passengers.
205.5 x 25.2 x 7.6m.
20 knots.
b. Wärtsilä, Helsinki,
Finland.
Yard No 396.
IMO 7218395.

Fred. Olsen Cruise Lines

Boudicca was built as *Royal Viking Sky* for the Norwegian Royal Viking Line and was lengthened by 28 metres in 1982. In 1987 she became part of the Norwegian Caribbean Line (Kloster Cruises) and was renamed *Sunward*. She was transferred to the Birka Line in 1992 and renamed *Birka Queen*, returning to Kloster in October 1992 until May of the following year. This was followed by a charter to Princess Cruises, when she was renamed *Golden Princess* and then to Star Cruises in 1996 as *Superstar Capricorn*.

In 1998 she was chartered to Hyundai Merchant Marine, cruising from Korea as *Hyundai Kumgang*. Following this charter she reverted to *Superstar Capricorn* before being laid up. Iberojet operated her as *Grand Latino* in 2004, prior to her being sold to Fred. Olsen who renamed her *Boudicca*, following a major overhaul during which she was re-engined by Blohm & Voss at Hamburg.

Britannia

2015
143,730 gt.
330 x 38.4 x 8.6m.
22 knots.
b. Fincantieri,
Monfalcone, Italy.
Yard No 6231.
IMO 9614036

P&O Cruises

In her first year **Britannia** cruised to and from the United Kingdom, the western Mediterranean, Norwegian fjords, the Atlantic islands and Iberia, western Europe, the Baltic, eastern and western Caribbean.

The ship and itineraries were designed specifically for British passengers. She has a capacity of 3,647 passengers who are able to enjoy the facilities on 15 public decks. In total there are 1,837 cabins comprising 64 suites, 1,313 balcony cabins and 460 inside cabins.

All the outside cabins have balconies and in response to the increasing number of solo travellers, **Britannia** has 15 single balcony cabins and 12 single inside cabins, which amounts to more single cabins than any other cruise ship.

Caribbean Princess

2004
112,894 gt.
3,112 passengers.
289 x 36 x 8m.
22½ knots.
b. Fincantieri,
Monfalcone, Italy.
Yard No 6067.
IMO 9215490.

Princess Cruises

Caribbean Princess was originally destined for the P&O Cruises fleet and was transferred to Princess Cruises prior to delivery. Princess Cruises was founded in 1965 by Stanley McDonald who chartered Canadian Pacific's cruise vessel *Princess Patricia* for cruises from Los Angeles to Mexico.

However the ship was unsuitable for tropical cruising and was replaced by the *Italia*, which also cruised to Alaska in 1969. She was followed by Costa's *Carla C* and the company was acquired by P&O in 1974, with the *Spirit of London* transferred to Princess, becoming *Sun Princess*. *Island Princess*, *Pacific Princess* and later *Sea Princess* were introduced with the line's first purpose-built ship *Royal Princess* joining the fleet in 1984. The Sitmar Line was acquired in 1988, whose fleet included the former Cunard vessels *Sylvania* and *Carinthia*, which became *Dawn Princess* and *Fair Princess* respectively, and *Fairsky* was renamed *Sky Princess*. *Star Princess, Crown Princess* and *Regal Princess* joined the fleet and P&O Princess Cruises was formed on 23 October 2000. In 2003 the company merged with the Carnival Corporation. By 2015 the Princess fleet comprised 18 cruise ships.

Carnival Legend

2002
85,942 gt.
2,132passengers
292.5 x 32.2 x 7.8m.
22 knots.
b. Kvaerner Masa
Yards, Helsinki,
Finland.
Yard No 501.
IMO 9224726

Carnival Cruise Lines

Carnival Legend diverted to Liverpool because of bad weather in the North Sea in September 2013.

Carnival Cruise Lines was formed by Ted Arison in 1972 with the *Empress of Canada*, which he renamed *Mardi Gras* for cruising out of Miami. She was followed by *Carnival* and *Festival* and their first new ship *Tropicale*, in 1982. *Holiday* followed in 1985, *Jubilee* the following year and *Celebration* in 1987. *Fantasy* came into service in 1990, *Ecstasy* in 1991, *Sensation* in 1993 and *Fascination* the following year. *Imagination* was introduced in 1995, *Inspiration* in 1996 and *Carnival Destiny*, the first passenger vessel to exceed 100,000 tons, joined the fleet in 1996. Cunard Line was taken in 1998 and Costa Line in 2000, *Elation* and *Paradise* entered service in 1998, *Carnival Triumph* in 1999 and *Carnival Victory* in 2000. *Carnival Legend* debuted in 2002 and *Carnival Glory* in 2003, with *Carnival Miracle* and *Carnival Valour* in 2004 and *Carnival Liberty* in 2005. *Carnival Freedom* followed in 2007, *Carnival Splendour* in 2008 and *Carnival Dream* in 2009. *Carnival Magic* was introduced in 2011 and *Carnival Breeze* the following year.

Caronia

1973
24,492 gt.
677 passengers.
191.1 x 25 x 8.2m.
21 knots.
b. Swan Hunter
Shipbuilders, Wallsend
on Tyne.
Yard No 39.
IMO 7214715

Cunard Line

Seen at anchor in the river, **Caronia** was built as **Vistafjord** for the Norwegian America Line (Den Norske Amerikalinje A/S) for service between Oslo and New York. She was sold to the Cunard Line in 1983 and entered service with them as **Vistafjord**. However she was renamed **Caronia** in 1999 at a ceremony at Liverpool Landing Stage and operated cruises from Southampton for the British cruise market.

In 2004 she was acquired by Saga Cruises, and following a major overhaul she joined their fleet as **Saga Ruby**. In January 2014 she was sold for $14 million to Millennium View Limited at Singapore to be used as a floating hotel in Burma, and was renamed **Oasia**.

Celebrity Infinity

2001
90,940 gt.
2,170 passengers
294 x 32.2 x 8.2m.
24 knots.
b. Chantiers de l'Atlantique, St Nazaire, France.
Yard No S31.
IMO 9189421

Celebrity Infinity was the second of the Millennium class and was delivered as *Infinity*. She is seen swinging in the river off the Cruise Terminal on a "Round Britain" cruise in 2015.

Celebrity Silhouette

2011
122,210 gt.
2,850 passengers.
315 x 36.8 x 8.3m.
22 knots.
b. J Meyer, Papenburg, Germany.
Yard No 679.
IMO 9451094

Celebrity Silhouette is the fourth vessel of the Solstice class and is shown on an evening departure from the Cruise Terminal.

Celebrity Cruises

Celebrity Cruises was formed in 1988 as a subsidiary of the Chandris Group, to provide a cruise service to Bermuda. The Chandris interest in Celebrity Cruises was sold to Royal Caribbean International in 1997. In 2007/8 all ships were renamed with the Celebrity prefix and *Celebrity Solstice* was delivered in October 2008. *Galaxy* was transferred to the TUI Cruises fleet and was renamed *Mein Schiff*. *Celebrity Mercury* became *Mein Schiff 2*, *Celebrity Silhouette* was delivered in 2011 and *Celebrity Reflection* the following year.

Late in 2014 it was announced that an order would be placed for two 2,900 passenger vessels to be marketed under the name EDGE. These vessels will be delivered between 2018 and 2020.

Clipper Adventurer

1975
4,376 gt.
122 passengers.
100 x 16.2 x 4.7m.
14 knots.
b. Brodogradiliste Titovo, Kraljevica, Yugoslavia.
Yard No 408.
IMO 7391422

Quark Expeditions

In 1991 Lars Wikander and Mike McDowell founded Quark Expeditions to specialise in expeditions to the Arctic and Antarctic on board purpose-built vessels. Quark Expeditions became part of the TUI Travel Group of companies in 2007.

In August 1991 they organised the first tourism transit of the Northeast Passage across northern Russia and in November 1997, the first circumnavigation of Antarctica for commercial passengers. *Clipper Adventurer* was built as *Alla Tarasova*, which was one of eight ships built for the Murmansk Shipping Company. She was rebuilt as a cruise ship in 1997 for Clipper Cruise Line, which became part of First Choice Travel and renamed *Clipper Adventurer*. In 2012 she became *Sea Adventurer*, managed by Fleetpro Ocean, Miami, Florida, USA.

We see her outward bound in the Mersey.

Crown Princess

2006
113,651 gt.
3,082 passengers.
288.6 x 36 x 8.5m.
22½ knots.
b. Fincantieri,
Monfalcone, Italy.
Yard No 6100. Forward
end of hull built at
Fincantieri yard at
Genoa
Yard No 1100.
IMO 9293399.

Princess Cruises

Crown Princess is a member of the "Grand" class of vessels and she sailed from New York on her maiden voyage on 14 June 2006. In July 2006 she was involved in a serious accident where 14 crew and passengers were injured, but happily there was no loss of life.

She is escorted by a Smit tug as she leaves the Cruise Terminal on a "Round Britain" cruise.

Crystal Cruises

This company was formed in 1988 as a wholly owned subsidiary of the parent company, Nippon Yusen Kaisha (NYK Line). *Crystal Harmony* was transferred to NYK in 2005 and renamed *Asuka II* to cater for the Japanese cruise market, and replaced the original vessel of the same name. The company is known as a luxury cruise line and operates two vessels, *Crystal Symphony* and *Crystal Serenity*. It was announced on 3 March 2015 that NYK was selling Crystal Cruises to Genting, Hong Kong, the owners of Star Cruises and that a new ship would be built for Crystal Cruises.

Crystal Serenity
2003
68,870 gt.   250 x 32.2 x 7.6m.   22 knots.
b. Chantiers de l'Atlantique, St Nazaire, France.
Yard No H32.
IMO 9243667.

Crystal Serenity was christened by Dame Julie Andrews and is shown leaving the Cruise Terminal on a sunny June evening. She sailed on her maiden voyage from Southampton to northern Europe on 7 July 2003.

Crystal Symphony
1995
51,044 gt.   238 x 30.2 x 7.6m.   22 knots.
b. Kvaerner Masa Yards, Turku, Finland.
Yard No 1323.
IMO 9066667

Crystal Symphony was christened by actress Angela Lansbury and is seen anchored in the Mersey off Albert Dock, prior to the opening of the Cruise Terminal at Liverpool Pier Head. In 2010 she operated in the Indian Ocean, Red Sea, Mediterranean, British Isles, Baltic and the Arctic Circle.

Deutschland

1998
22,496 gt.
576 passengers.
175.3 x 23 x 5.8m.
20 knots.
b. Howaldtswerke-
Deutsche Werft,
Hamburg, Germany.
Yard No 328.
IMO 9141807

Deilmann Cruises

While berthed at the Norwegian port of Eidfjord on 23 May 2010 she suffered a serious engine room fire which was brought under control by the closure of the fire doors. The passengers travelled home and the ship was towed to Hamburg for repairs. On 15 January 2012 she grounded briefly in the Beagle Channel off South America. In 2012 the German Olympic Committee chartered the **Deutschland** as an accommodation ship and she was berthed in London Docks during the Summer Olympics. **Deutschland** was handed over to her new American owners, the Absolute Nevada in May 2015.

On 31 May it was announced that Plantours would be chartering the ship for four sailings between 9 June and 29 July while their cruise ship **Hamburg** was under repair. Her funnel was painted into Plantours yellow branding and in July and August 2015 she cruised in the North Sea, Norwegian fjords, Greenland, Faroes and the Shetland Islands.

The company was declared bankrupt in 2015.

Discovery

1972
20,216 gt.
698 passengers.
168.7 x 24.6 x 7.5m.
18 knots.
b. Rheinstahl
Nordseewerke, Emden,
Germany.
Yard No 414.
IMO 7108514

Voyages of Discovery

Discovery was built as *Island Venture* and it was planned to operate a two-ship service, with *Sea Venture* from New York to Bermuda by Flagship Cruises. However only one ship was needed to sustain the route and *Island Venture* was chartered to Princess Cruises as *Island Princess* in 1972.

She was sold to Ringcroft Investment and chartered to Hyundai Merchant Marine in 1999, and renamed *Hyundai Pungak*. Purchased by Orient Lines in 2001, she was renamed *Platinum*, operating from South America in winter and Voyages of Discovery in the summer months.

From 2004 she was marketed by Discovery World Cruises and later Voyages of Discovery until 2012, when she was chartered to Cruise and Maritime Voyages. She was withdrawn in 2014, renamed *Amen* for her voyage to the shipbreakers, and beached at Alang on 8 December that year.

The photograph shows her getting underway on departure from the Cruise Terminal.

Doulos
1914
6,804 gt.
130.4 x 16.5 x 5.6m.
13 knots.
b. Newport News
Shipbuilding and Dry
Dock Company.
Yard No 176.
IMO 5119105

Operation Mobilisation

She was built as **Medina** for the Mallory Steamship Company's service from the east coast of America to the Gulf of Mexico. In 1948 she was sold and converted to an emigrant ship for the United Kingdom to Australia trade. She was renamed **Roma** and was acquired by the Costa Line in 1952, becoming **Franca C** to operate between Italy and South America, following conversion to a motor ship.

In 1959 she was transferred to cruising duties and was re-engined in 1970. In 1977 she was renamed **Doulos** for Operation Mobilisation and used as a missionary ship and floating bookshop. From 2010 she was classed as a restaurant ship in Singapore. However, in 2013 it was announced that she would be refurbished at Batam, Indonesia, but it was later stated that the plans to convert her to a restaurant had been cancelled, and that she would be removed from the water for use on land in a dry berth.

Edinburgh Castle

1966
30,567 gt.
217.5 x 29.4m.
b. Fincantieri,
Monfalcone, Italy.
Yard No 1884.
IMO 6502024.

Direct Cruises

She was built as **Eugenio C**, becoming **Eugenio Costa** in 1987 and **Edinburgh Castle** in 1997 for Direct Cruises. Direct Holidays were one of Britain's direct sell companies and were backed by the Royal Bank of Scotland, with full membership of the Association of British Travel Agents (ABTA).

Cruises from Liverpool were offered to the Mediterranean, Atlantic islands, Iceland, Greenland and the Norwegian fjords. In 2000 she was sold and renamed **Big Red Boat II**, **Red Boat** in 2004 and **Big Red Boat II** again the following year.

She arrived at Alang on 1 June 2005 to be broken up.

Europa

1999
28,890 gt.
400 passengers.
198.6 x 24 x 6.1m.
21 knots.
b. Kvaerner Masa
Yards, Helsinki,
Finland.
Yard No 495.
IMO 9183855

Hapag Lloyd Cruises

On the morning of Monday 11 August 2014 *Europa* was due to berth at the Cruise Terminal on a cruise. However, *AIDAcara* was still at the stage because of strong winds in the Irish Sea the previous night.

As the winds had abated overnight *AIDAcara* was able to leave Liverpool to enable *Europa* to dock. It was a long time since there were two large passenger vessels in the Mersey off the Pier Head.

Funchal

1961
9,563 gt.
469 passengers.
152.7 x 19 x 6.3m.
17 knots.
b. Helsingør Shipyard,
Denmark.
Yard No 353.
IMO 5124162

Portuscale Cruises

Funchal was built for Empresa Insulana de Navegacão, Lisbon, Portugal for the Lisbon to Madeira, Azores and Canary Islands route, and she was occasionally used as the Portuguese Presidential Yacht.

In 1972 her machinery was replaced with diesel engines and two years later was operating for Companhia Portuguesa de Transportes Maritimos. She was sold to Great Warwick of Panama in 1985 and managed by Arcalia Shipping. In 2007, 2009 and in 2010/11 she undertook various major overhauls.

Hanseatic
1991
8,378 gt.
175 passengers.
122.7 x 18 x 4.8m.
16 knots.
b. Rauma Yards,
Rauma, Finland.
Yard No 306.
IMO 9000168

Hapag Lloyd Cruises

She was built as the **Society Adventurer** for Society Expedition Cruises but was laid up until March, 1993, and was then chartered to Hanseatic Tours, becoming **Hanseatic**. The company was acquired by Hapag-Lloyd in 1996, and **Hanseatic** was employed on cruises to Greenland and Antarctica.

A serious fire broke out while she was in drydock at the Bredo Shipyard in Bremerhaven on 13 June 2013 and several cruises were cancelled in June and July that year. She is classed as the only five-star expedition cruise ship worldwide in the *Berlitz Complete Guide to Cruising and Cruise Ships*.

Hebridean Princess

1964
2,112 gt.
49 passengers.
71.6 x 13.3 x 2.7m.
14½ knots.
b. Hall, Russell &
Company Limited,
Aberdeen.
Yard No 912.
IMO 6409351.

Hebridean Island Cruises

Hebridean Princess was built as the car ferry **Columba** for David MacBrayne's services in Scotland. The company was merged with the Caledonian Steam Packet in 1973, becoming Caledonian MacBrayne, which was in turn purchased by the All Leisure Group in 2009.

Columba was sold to Leisure and Marine Holdings (Hebridean Island Cruises) in 1988, and converted into a cruise ship the following year by George Prior Engineering at Great Yarmouth. After she had been in service for two years her car carrying facilities were removed and additional passenger cabins provided. In 1998 she was acquired by Hebridean Cruises plc and continued with her normal programme of cruises.

Hebridean Princess was chartered by Her Majesty the Queen from 21 July to 29 July 2006 and operated a cruise around the Scottish Islands with members of the royal family aboard to celebrate her 80th birthday.

Hebridean Spirit 1991 4,200 gt. 80 passengers. 90.6 x 15.3 x 3.6m. 15 ½ knots.
b. Nuovi Cantieri Apuania, Marina di Carrara, Italy. Yard No 1145. IMO 8802870

Hebridean Island Cruises

She was built as **Renaissance Six** for Renaissance Cruises and was sold to Sun Cruises in 1998, becoming **Sun Viva 2**, and **Megastar Capricorn** in 2000. The following year she was acquired by Hebridean Island Cruises but when the company was placed in administration she was sold and renamed **Sunrise** in 2009. We see her here berthed at the Isle of Man landing stage, which preceded the Cruise Terminal.

Horizon

1990
47,427 gt.
1,442 passengers.
208 x 29 x 7.4m.
21 knots.
b. Meyer, Papenburg,
Germany.
Yard No 619.
IMO 8807088

Croisières de France

The company was formed in 2007. It is a subsidiary of the Royal Caribbean Cruise Line and offers cruises mainly to the French market. She is seen here leaving the Cruise Terminal in 2015, after the passengers had spent the day in Liverpool.

Horizon was built for Celebrity Cruises and became *Island Star*, operating for Island Cruises in 2005. Following the demise of Island Cruises in 2009 she was transferred to Pullmantur and renamed *Pacific Dream*. Operating in the Mediterranean in 2010 she became *Horizon* and was transferred to Croisières de France in 2012.

Le Boreal
2010
10,944 gt.
264 passengers.
142 x 18 x 4.6m
16 knots.
b. Fincantieri, Ancona, Italy.
Yard No 6192.
IMO 9502506

Ponant Cruises

Ponant Cruises was established in 1988 as Compagnie du Ponant and operates *Le Ponant, Le Boreal, L' Austral, Le Soleal* and *Le Lyrial*. Ponant Cruises operates throughout the world from the Mediterranean to Antarctica and Greenland.

On 18 November 2015 she suffered a major engine room fire which caused a loss of power. She was near Cape Dolphin, the northerly point of East Falkland, Falkland Islands. Two Sea King Royal Air Force Search and Rescue helicopters, a C - 130 Hercules and a Voyager aircraft were sent to the scene. HMS Clyde and two Dutch tugs assisted and the passengers and crew were taken to the Falkland Islands.

Le Boreal is described as a "super-yacht, which is sleek in design" and was awarded the prize of Best New Ship of the Year in 2010 when she was launched.

Maasdam

1993
55,575 gt.
1,258 passengers.
219.2 x 30.8 x 7.7m.
20 knots.
b. Fincantieri,
Monfalcone, Italy.
Yard No 5882.
IMO 8919257

Holland America Line

Maasdam lifts her anchor after spending the day off Cammell Laird's shipyard with Mersey ferries acting as tenders for the passengers. This was prior to the opening of the designated berth at the Liverpool Cruise Terminal and the strong winds caused many problems for the crew of *Maasdam* during the day.

She was ordered with sisters *Statendam* and *Ryndam* in 1989 and all were fitted with additional ballast tanks to enable them to meet the SOLAS 90 International Convention for the Safety of Life at Sea stability requirements. The three ships were also fitted with articulated "Hinze" flap rudders to improve their manoeuvrability. It was claimed that the class was the most technically advanced design when they were delivered.

Maasdam received an extensive overhaul in 2006 at Freeport, Bahamas. In recent years she has been based at Fort Lauderdale during the winter months and sails from Boston to Europe, Canadian ports and New England in the summer.

Marco Polo

1965
22,080 gt.
800 passengers.
176.3 x 23.6 x 8.2m.
19½ knots.
b. Mathias Thesen
Werft, Wismar,
Germany.
Yard No 126.
IMO 6417097

Cruise and Maritime Voyages

Marco Polo is advertised as "a cruise ship with her handsome traditional profile, beautiful teak decks and distinctive blue hull, as a classic ocean liner. She reflects a truly intimate cruise experience and is fully stabilised and air conditioned."

She was delivered as **Aleksandr Pushkin**, one of five ships built for the Black Sea Shipping Company and the Baltic Shipping Company, and was operated on the service from Leningrad to Montreal. In 1975 she was employed on cruising duties and was chartered to Transocean in 1979. She was operating for the Far Eastern Shipping Company in 1985 and carried out charters for CTC Lines from Australia.

In 1991 she was owned by Orient Lines and later completed a major overhaul. She was acquired by Global Maritime in 2007 and chartered to Transocean Tours. From 2010 she has been operating for Cruise and Maritime Voyages.

Marina

2011
66,084 gt.
1,250 passengers.
239.3 x 32.2 x 7.6m
20 knots.
b. Fincantieri, Sestri, Italy.
Yard 6194.
IMO 9438066

Oceania Cruises

Oceania Cruises was formed in 2002 by Frank Del Rio, Joe Watters and Bob Binder as the world's largest upper premium cruise line.

When Renaissance Cruises failed in 2001 Oceania Cruises chartered **R One**, **R Two** and **R Five** and later purchased the three vessels. **R One** was renamed **Insignia**, **R Two** became **Regatta** and **R Five** was named **Nautica**.

Marina and **Riviera** were built at Genoa and introduced into the fleet in 2011 and 2012 respectively.

We see her off New Brighton as she heads up the River Mersey.

Mein Schiff 2
1997
77,302 gt.
1,912 passengers.
263.9 x 32.2 x 7.7m.
21½ knots.
b. J Meyer, Papenburg, Germany.
Yard No 639.
IMO 9106302

Mein Schiff 4
2015
99,500 gt.
2,506 passengers.
293.2 x 35.8 x 8m.
22 knots.
b. STX, Finland.
Yard No 1384.
IMO 9678408

TUI Cruises

Mein Schiff 2 was built as *Mercury* for Celebrity Cruises. In 2008 she became *Celebrity Mercury* and was transferred to TUI in 2011 and renamed *Mein Schiff 2*. On a cruise programme based at Charleston, South Carolina in 2010 the *Mercury* reported a serious outbreak of norovirus, involving around 500 passengers. TUI Cruises is a German Joint Venture between the Royal Caribbean Cruise Lines and TUI AG and was established in 2008.

Mein Schiff 4 departed on 6 June 2015 from Kiel, her home port, on her maiden voyage to the eastern Baltic.

Her main winter voyages are to the Canary Islands, Morocco and Madeira.

She is seen here at the Cruise Terminal with the ferry *Snowdrop* in the foreground.

MSC Magnifica

2010
92,128 gt.
2,518 passengers.
293 x 32.2 x 7.9m.
22 knots.
b. STX Europe, St Nazaire, France.
Yard No T32.
IMO 9387085

MSC Crociere

MSC Cruises is the world's largest privately owned cruise company, which employs 15,500 people worldwide and has offices in 45 countries. It is part of the Mediterranean Shipping Company, which is the world's second largest shipping operator.

Lauro Lines began operating in the 1960s with the **Achille Lauro**, and in 1989 the Mediterranean Shipping Company acquired Lauro and it was renamed Lauro Cruises. The company became MSC Cruises in 1995 and it is now the fourth largest cruise company in the world.

Nippon Maru
1990
22,472 gt.
368 passengers
166.6 x 23.6 x 6.6m.
18 knots.
b. Mitsubishi Heavy
Industries.
Yard No 1188.
IMO 8817631

Mitsui OSK Passenger Lines

Nippon Maru now operates for part of the year under the Southeast Asian and Japanese Youth Programme. The aim of the programme is to foster friendship and greater understanding among young people from Japan and other countries in the region.

MOL (Mitsui OSK Lines, Limited) has one of the largest shipping fleets in the world. In 1964 Japan's shipping industry undertook a major consolidation, with mergers creating six companies -- Mitsui O.S.K. Lines, Ltd. (MOL) by a merger of OSK Line and Mitsui Steamship, Japan Line, Ltd. (JL) by a merger of Nitto Shosen and Daido Kaiun, and Yamashita-Shinnihon Steamship Co., Ltd. (YSL) by a merger of Yamashita Kisen and Shinnihon Kisen. Another re-organisation took place in 1999 with the Navix Line.

Ocean Countess

1976
16,795 gt.
814 passengers.
163.6 x 22.8 x 5.8m.
18½ knots.
b. Burmeister & Wain,
Copenhagen, Denmark.
Yard N ̊858.
IMO 73̊ ̊561

Cruise and Maritime Voyages

Ocean Countess was built as *Cunard Countess* for the Cunard Line and became *Awani Dream 2* in 1996, *Olympic Countess* in 1998, *Olympia Countess* in 2002, *Ocean Countess* in 2004, *Lili Marleen* in 2005, *Ocean Countess* again in 2006, *Ruby* and *Ocean Countess* in 2007. She operated a charter to Cruise and Maritime in 2010/11 and was laid up in 2013. On 30 November 2013 she was badly damaged when a serious fire broke out on her at Chalkis in Greece. She was declared a total loss and departed Chalkis under tow for Aliaga on 7 March 2014.

Prominent in the background is the Wheel of Liverpool. Built in 2010, it has 42 fully enclosed air-conditioned capsules and offers spectacular views over the city and away to the Welsh mountains in the distance.

Ocean Majesty
1966
10,417 gt.
500 passengers.
130.6 x 19.2 x 5.4m.
20 knots.
b. Union Naval de Levante, Valencia, Spain.
Yard No 93.
IMO 6602898

Majestic International Cruises

Built as the car ferry **Juan March** for Compania Trasmediterranea, to operate on the Barcelona - Palma, Majorca, service, and Barcelona to the Canary Islands. She was sold to Greece in 1985, becoming **Sol Christiana** for the Piraeus to Crete, Rhodes, Cyprus and Israel service.

In 1986 she was sold and renamed **Kypros Star** and **Ocean Majesty** three years later. Operating on charter to Epirotiki in 1994 she became **Olympia**, and **Homeric** the following year. In 1995 she was on charter to Page & Moy as **Ocean Majesty**, and continued to provide cruises for them up to 2009, when she was transferred to Apex Tours of Turkey.

Olvia
1976
15,791 gt.
500 passengers.
156.3 x 21.8 x 5.9m.
21 knots.
b. Wärtsilä, Turku,
Finland.
Yard No 1223.
IMO 7359498

Kaalbye Shipping Company

Olvia arriving in Langton lock when on charter to the Peaceboat Organisation. She was built for the Black Sea Shipping Company as *Kareliya*, becoming *Leonid Brezhnev* in 1982, *Kareliya* in 1989, *Olvia* in 1998, *Neptune* in 2004, *CT Neptune* in 2005, *Neptune* in 2006 for Neptune Cruises and *Starry Metropolis* in 2011, when purchased by Hopewin Ship Management/Metropolis Cruise Company Limited, Kowloon, Hong Kong.

The Kaalbye Shipping Company is a Ukrainian company which is registered in the British Virgin Islands. It has always been associated with the operation of cargo ships. It was given permission to operate passenger vessels in May 1998.

Prinsendam
1988
39,051 gt.
835 passengers.
204 x 28.9 x 7.2m.
21 knots.
b. Wärtsilä, Turku,
Finland.
Yard No 1296.
IMO 8700280

Holland America Line

Prinsendam was built as *Royal Viking Sun* for the Royal Viking Line. She was acquired by Cunard Line in 1994, retaining her original name. She undertook world voyages for Cunard and was very popular with both passengers and crew.

Following the merger of Cunard and the Carnival Corporation she was transferred to Seabourn in 1999, becoming *Seabourn Sun* following an extensive refit. In 2002 she was given the name *Prinsendam*, as a member of the Holland America Line fleet after another major refit.

Prinsendam, *Veendam* and *Amsterdam* are the only three Holland America ships that visit Antarctica and she is small enough to be able to navigate the Kiel Canal. On 22 March 2012, while on route to Portimao, Portugal, she rescued eight fishermen from their sinking vessel.

Queen Elizabeth

2010
90,901 gt.
2,014 passengers.
294 x 32.3 x 7.9m.
22 knots.
b. Fincantieri,
Monfalcone, Italy.
Yard No 6187.
IMO 9477438

Cunard Line

Queen Elizabeth was laid down on 2 July 2009 and launched on 5 January 2010. She was christened by Her Majesty Queen Elizabeth at Southampton on 11 October 2010, prior to sailing on her maiden voyage the following day.

She is a "Vista" class cruise ship and is the second largest vessel constructed for the Cunard Line. She is very similar to but slightly larger than *Queen Victoria*, which is due to her more vertical stern. The *Queen Elizabeth* and *Queen Victoria* have been built with a stronger bow for transatlantic crossings. The "Vista" class is a class of Panamax type cruise ships and they are operated by Holland America Line, P&O Cruises, Cunard Line and Costa Cruises. The ships are equipped with diesel-electric engines and an Azipod propulsion system.

In the foreground is the tug *MSC Victory*, usually to be found assisting ships in the Manchester Ship Canal.

Queen of the Isles

1965
515 gt.
300 passengers
48m x 9m
13 knots.
b. Charles Hill & Sons,
Bristol.
IMO 6501783.

The Isles of Scilly Steamship Company

Queen of the Isles operated cruises from Liverpool to Llandudno and Menai Bridge, North Wales. She became *Olovaha* in 1970 and *Gulf Explorer* in 1982, *Queen of the Isles* in 1987, *Island Princess* in 1994 and *Western Queen* in 1994.

She was beached at Ranadi, following Cyclone Justin in 1997 and declared a total loss.

Queen Mary 2
2003
148,528 gt.
2,620 passengers.
345 x 41 x 10.3m.
29 knots.
b. Chantiers de l'Atlantique, St Nazaire, France.
Yard No G32.
IMO 9241061

Cunard Line

Queen Mary 2 was laid down on 4 July 2002 and was christened on 8 January 2004 by Her Majesty the Queen. She was built as a transatlantic ocean liner/cruise ship and on delivery became flagship of the Cunard Line. At the time of her construction she was the longest passenger vessel ever built.

Her dual role as cruise ship and ocean liner meant that she required high quality steel and a more powerful propulsion system to enable her to maintain the trans-Atlantic schedules. Her sea trials took place on 25-29 September and 7-11 November 2003, and her final construction was marred by an accident at the shipyard. However she was completed on schedule and was handed over to the Cunard Line at Southampton on 26 December 2003. *Queen Mary 2* sailed on her maiden voyage from Southampton to Fort Lauderdale on 12 January 2004, commanded by Captain Ronald Warwick, who had previously been in command the *Queen Elizabeth 2*.

She is seen berthed at the Cruise Terminal on 4 July 2015 preparing to sail on the 175th Anniversary Crossing of the Atlantic to Halifax, Boston and New York.

Queen Victoria
2007
90,049 gt.
1,980 passengers.
294 x 32.3 x 7.9m.
22 knots.
b. Fincantieri,
Monfalcone, Italy.
Yard No 6127.
IMO 9320556

Cunard Line

Queen Victoria's keel was laid on 12 May 2006 with 80 prefabricated steel blocks, each complete with interior structure, cabling and ducts, and each weighing 325 tons. The hull was floated out on 15 January 2007 and she sailed from the Port of Venice on 24 August 2007 on her sea trials, arriving at Southampton on 7 December.

She was christened on 10 December by Camilla, Duchess of Cornwall, and sailed on her maiden voyage to northern Europe the following day. This was followed by a cruise to the Canary Islands before she embarked on her first world cruise. The first leg of this voyage was in tandem with *Queen Elizabeth 2* across the Atlantic, and they met *Queen Mary 2* in New York. It was the first time the three vessels had been together. It was expected to be the only time they would ever meet but a rendezvous did occur again on 22 April 2008 at Southampton, following a change in *QE2*'s schedule. *Queen Victoria* is also a "Vista" class vessel and is similar to the *Queen Elizabeth* but is slightly smaller.

The Cunard Line are proud that Liverpool will always be part of their history and in 2015 celebrated 175 years of sailing with three key anniversary cruises, which included a visit to Liverpool. **Queen Mary 2** arrived on the river on 24th May for her first overnight stay in the city, and the following morning she sailed from the Cruise Terminal to meet **Queen Elizabeth** and **Queen Victoria** at the mouth of the river. **Queen Elizabeth** arrived from Kirkwall in the Orkney Islands and **Queen Victoria** from Guernsey. The three vessels sailed up the Mersey and performed a synchronised manoeuvre of 180 degrees off the Pier Head at Liverpool, as the Red Arrows aerobatic team flew in formation above the river from the Wirral side and over Liverpool.

The Three Queens spectacular was witnessed by tens of thousands of people on both sides of the Mersey and also from dozens of small craft, yachts, tugs and the famous Mersey ferries. *Queen Mary 2* was the first vessel to break formation when she sailed slowly past the Three Graces at the Pier Head to continue her voyage to Guernsey in brilliant sunshine. *Queen Elizabeth* then proceeded to the Cruise Terminal where she would berth until sailing later that evening to the accompaniment of a firework display. As she left *Queen Victoria* took her berth at the Cruise Terminal departing from the river the following afternoon.

Quest for Adventure

1981
18,627grt.
466 passengers.
164.3 x 22 x 6.1m.
b. Howaldtswerke-
Deutsche Werft,
Hamburg, Germany.
Yard No 165.
IMO 8000214

Saga Cruises

Quest for Adventure was built as the *Astor* for the Hadag Cruise Line and was sold to the South African Marine Corporation for a liner service from Cape Town to the United Kingdom. She was sold in 1985 and renamed *Arkona*, *Astoria* in 2002, *Saga Pearl II* in 2010, *Quest for Adventure* in 2012 and *Saga Pearl II* in 2013.

Rotterdam
1997
61,849 gt.
1,404 passengers.
237.9 x 32.2 x 7.5m.
22½ knots.
b. Fincantieri, Marghera
Yard, Venice, Italy.
Yard No 5980.
IMO 9122552

Holland America Line

Rotterdam was launched on 21 December 1996 and is the sixth Holland America Line vessel to bear the name. In the summer of 2011, *Rotterdam* conducted Holland America Line's first transatlantic crossing since 1971, making a single trip both eastbound and westbound.

She normally operates in Europe during the summer months and South America in the winter, and from 2012 she has been based in Rotterdam. In 2014 she circumnavigated South America for 88 days from 12 November to 20 December.

She completed the voyage by sailing from Cape Town to Luderitz, Walvis Bay, Luanda, Cape Verde, the Canary Islands, Agadir, Casablanca, Tangier, Cadiz, Vigo, Lisbon and Southampton.

Royal Princess

2013
142,714 gt.
3,560 passengers.
330 x 38.4 x 8.6m.
22 knots.
b. Fincantieri,
Monfalcone, Italy.
Yard No 6223.
IMO 9584712

Princess Cruises

Royal Princess is a "Royal" class cruise ship and was christened by Her Royal Highness The Duchess of Cambridge on 13 June 2013. She is the third ship to sail for Princess under that name.

The Mersey Ferry *Snowdrop* welcomes *Royal Princess* to the Mersey, off Seacombe prior to her swinging in the river to berth at the Cruise Terminal in 2015. *Snowdrop* sports a mock version of the 'Dazzle' livery used to disguise ships in World War 1.

R Seven

2000
30,277 gt.
716 passengers.
181 x 25.5 x 6m.
18 knots.
b. Chantiers de l'Atlantique, St Nazaire, France.
Yard No X31.
IMO 9210218

Renaissance Cruises

A very early morning arrival for **R Seven** in the Mersey, following a last-minute diversion from Belfast. She berthed at Langton Dock and continued her "Round Britain" cruise later that day.

When the company was placed into administration **R Seven** was laid up at Gibraltar and was sold to Cruiseinvest and later chartered to Delphin Seereisen, becoming **Delphin Renaissance**. She was renamed **Blue Moon** in 2006 and **Azamara Quest** the following year.

Ruby Princess

2008
113,561 gt.
3,084 passengers.
290 x 36 x 8.5m.
22½ knots.
b. Fincantieri, Monfalcone, Italy.
Yard No 6150.
IMO 9378462

Princess Cruises

A rare lunchtime arrival by **Ruby Princess** as it is normal for cruise ships to berth early in the morning and spend the day moored at the Cruise Terminal to allow passengers to visit Liverpool or travel throughout the local area.

Ruby Princess is a "Grand" class cruise ship and is similar to **Crown Princess** and **Emerald Princess**. She has been based at Los Angeles, offering sailings to Hawaii and Fort Lauderdale, sailing to the Caribbean Islands.

Saga Rose

1965
24,528 gt.
587 passengers.
188.9 x 24.5 x 8.3m.
20 knots.
b. Forges et Chantiers
de La Méditerranée, La
Seyne, France.
Yard No 1366.
IMO 6416043

Saga Holidays

Sagafjord was built for Den Norske Amerikalinje A/S (Norwegian America Line) for their service from Oslo to New York. *Sagafjord* sailed on her maiden voyage from Oslo to New York on 2 October 1965 and also operated as a cruise ship in the winter months. Norwegian America Cruises was formed in 1980 and *Sagafjord* was sold to the Cunard Line in 1983, and operated with them under her original name.

She was chartered to Transocean in 1996, becoming *Gripsholm*. She was purchased by the Saga Line in 1997, renamed *Saga Rose* and operated by them until October 2009.

She was withdrawn from service as she did not meet with SOLAS 2010 regulations and set off from Gibraltar on 21 February 2010, where she had been laid up since her final cruise with Saga Cruises. She anchored for a few days off Shanghai and docked at Jiangyin on 29 May and was subsequently broken up. She holds the record for the most world cruises by a ship with 44 completed as *Sagafjord*.

Saga Sapphire

1981
37,049 gt.
706 passengers.
199.6 x 28.5 x 8.4m.
21 knots.
b. Bremer Vulkan, Vegesack, Germany.
Yard No 1001.
IMO 7822457

Saga Cruises

She was built as **Europa** for Hapag-Lloyd and was sold to Star Cruises and briefly named **Megastar Asia**, later **Superstar Europe** and **Superstar Aires** in 1999, **Superstar Europe** in 2004, **Holiday Dream** in 2006, **Bleu De France** in 2008 and **Saga Sapphire** in 2012.

Seabourn Pride

1988
9,975 gt.
208 passengers.
133.8 x 19 x 5.2m.
19 knots.
b. Schichau Seebeckwerft, Bremerhaven, Germany.
Yard No 1065.
IMO 8707343

Seabourn Cruise Line

Seabourn Pride berthed at the Cruise Terminal.

She was sold to Windstar Cruises in 2013 and delivered the following year, becoming **Star Pride**.

Seabourn Pride, **Seabourn Spirit** and **Seabourn Legend** were all purchased by Windstar and were integrated into the fleet. The acquisition of the three ships doubled the size of the Windstar fleet which comprised **Wind Spirit**, **Wind Star** and **Wind Surf**.

Seven Seas Voyager

2003
42,363 gt.
206.5 x 28.8 x 7.1m.
700 passengers.
20 knots.
b. Hull built by Cantieri Nav. Visentini, Donada, Italy, under sub-contract to T Mariotti at Genoa.
Yard No MAR001.
IMO 9247144

Regent Seven Seas Cruises

The company was formally Radisson Seven Seas Cruises, which was a joint venture between the American group Carlson and Vlassov (V Ships of Monaco). In 1992 Carlson established Diamond Cruise Line, which later became Radisson Diamond Cruises to operate Radisson Diamond. Seven Seas Cruises and its vessel **Song of Flower** were later taken over with the company becoming Radisson Seven Seas Cruises. The **Paul Gauguin** was leased and the joint company was established in 1999 when **Seven Seas Navigator** was delivered.

The name was changed to Regent Seven Seas Cruises in 2006 and two years later it was acquired by Apollo Management, under Prestige Cruises. **Seven Seas Voyager** was christened in Monaco by Barbara Carlson in the presence of Prince Albert II. She is seen anchored in the Mersey opposite Woodside at Birkenhead with the Mersey ferry **Royal Iris of the Mersey**, acting as a tender. The photograph was taken from the viewing balcony at St Mary's Church tower, near Cammell Laird's shipyard, Birkenhead.

Silver Wind
1995
16,927 gt.
296 passengers.
155.8 x 21.4 x 5.3m.
20 knots.
b. Cantieri Navali
Visentini, Donada, Italy.
Yard No 776.
IMO 8903935

Silversea Cruises

Silver Wind berthed at the Isle of Man landing stage.

Silversea specialises in small luxury ships. The line is owned by the Lefebvres family of Rome. The itineraries include many ports with late night and overnight departures providing the passenger with more time to experience the local area and cultures. Silversea launched **Silver Cloud** in 1994 and **Silver Wind** in 1995, followed by the slightly larger sister ships, **Silver Shadow** and **Silver Whisper** in 2000 and 2001; and in 2009, Silversea's flagship **Silver Spirit**.

Song of Norway
1970
22,945 gt.
1,140 passengers.
194.3 x 24 x 6.7m.
20½ knots.
b. Wärtsilä, Helsinki, Finland.
Yard No 392.
IMO 7005190

Royal Caribbean Cruise Line

Song of Norway was built as part of an order for three similar cruise ships for the Royal Caribbean Cruise Line, and was lengthened during a major overhaul in 1980. She was acquired by Sun Cruises in 1997, becoming *Sundream* and *Dream Princes* in 2004, when she was sold to Tumaco Shipping. The following year she was operating for Caspi Cruises, offering cruises in the Mediterranean.

In 2006 she became *Dream, Clipper Pearl* in 2007 and *Clipper Pacific* in 2008, on charter to the Peaceboat Organisation. She was damaged in the Atlantic and put into New York, where she was detained by the U.S. Coastguard but was later allowed to continue her voyage. On arrival at Piraeus she suffered serious mechanical problems and the passengers were transferred to the *Mona Lisa*, which had been chartered by the Organisation. She became *Festival* and *Ocean Pearl* in 2009, *Formosa Queen* in 2012 and was broken up in China in 2013.

We see her berthed at the Isle of Man landing stage with the Royal Liver building prominent in the background.

Spirit of Adventure
1980
9,570 gt.
348 passengers.
139.3 x 17.5 x 4.8m
17 knots.
b. Howaldtswerke-
Deutsche Werft,
Hamburg, Germany.
Yard No 163
IMO 7904889.

Saga

Spirit of Adventure leaving Langton lock on a cruise to the Mediterranean.

She was built as **Berlin** for a consortium of German investors. In 1982 she was chartered by Blue Funnel for the Straits Steamship Company to replace the **Centaur** and renamed **Princess Mahsuri**. On completion of the charter in 1984 she reverted to **Berlin**. In 1986 she was lengthened by 17 metres in Germany and was operated by Deilmann until 2005 when she was chartered as **Orange Melody**. Following this charter she was purchased by Saga, becoming **Spirit of Adventure**, **FTI Berlin** in 2012 and **Berlin** in 2014.

S of the Seas

19
69
1,8 rs.
264 .
24 knots.
b. Chantiers de l'Atlantique, St Nazaire, France.
Yard No B31.
IMO 9070632

Royal Caribbean International

Splendour of the Seas anchored mid-river prior to the opening of the Cruise Terminal.

She is a "Vision" class ship, launched on 17 June 1995 and she sailed on her maiden voyage on 31 March the following year. In 2011 Royal Caribbean contracted the Spanish shipyard Navantia to carry out structural modifications, maintenance to the propellers, propeller shafts and rudder.

Southern Cross

1972
17,042 gt.
792 passengers.
163.3 x 22.8 x 6.5m.
17 knots.
b. Cantieri Navale del Tirreno e Riuniti, Italy.
Yard No 290.
IMO 7211517

CTC Cruise Lines

Southern Cross cruised from Liverpool to the Mediterranean in 1995. She was launched as **Spirit of London** and was the first P&O vessel to be built exclusively for cruising. Renamed **Sun Princess** in 1974, **Starship Majesty** in 1989, **Southern Cross** in 1995, **Flamenco** in 1997, **Elysian Flamenco** and **New Flamenco** in 2004, **Flamenco** again in 2008 and **Ocean Dream** in 2011. She was anchored in the Gulf of Siam, off Thailand in 2015 and capsized and sank in February 2016.

Sunbird

1982
37,773 gt.
1,450 passengers.
214.5 x 28.4 x 7m.
19 knots.
b. Wärtsilä, Helsinki,
Finland.
Yard No 431.
IMO 7927984

Airtours

Sunbird anchored in the Mersey following a major overhaul by Cammell Laird at Birkenhead.

She was built as *Song of America* for the Royal Caribbean Cruise Line and was sold to Airtours in 1999, becoming *Sunbird*. Airtours later became MyTravel and *Sunbird* was renamed *Thomson Destiny* in 2005 and *Celestyal Olympia* in 2012, then *Louis Olympia* in 2012 and *Celestyal Olympia* in 2014.

The World

2002
43,188grt.
330 passengers.
196.4 x 29.2 x 6.9m.
19 knots.
b. Bruce's Shipyard,
Landskrona, Sweden
and Fosen Yard at
Rissa, Norway.
Yard No 247.
IMO 9219331.

Residensea

The World is the largest private residential ship and since its launch has continuously circumnavigated the globe, spending time in ports, allowing residents to experience new destinations every few days. The ship has 165 individual homes and residents not only own their homes but also own the ship. The accommodation comprises 106 two and three bedroom apartments, 19 one and two bedroom studio apartments and 40 studios. Residents are involved in choosing the ship's itinerary and specialist guests and experts are invited on-board to advise residents on the different cultures, traditions, languages they will experience at each port of call.

The World's 2015 journey started at Singapore, before exploring the islands and cities of south-east Asia. She then proceeded to the Maldives and Seychelles and West Africa. From there she headed to Morocco, the Mediterranean, the United Kingdom, and Iceland, before arriving at Greenland and down the east coast of Canada and the United States to transit the Panama Canal and the west coast of South America, before another expedition to Antarctica.

Thomson Spirit
1983
33,930 gt.
1,254 passengers.
214.7 x 27.2 x 7.5m.
18 knots.
b. Chantiers de l'Atlantique, St Nazaire, France.
Yard No V27.
IMO 8024014

Thomson Cruises

Thomson Spirit was delivered to the Holland America Line as **Nieuw Amsterdam** and was sold to American Hawaii Cruises and renamed **Patriot** in 2000. She was the first of a pair of identical ships built at St Nazaire for the Holland America Line. While under construction a fire destroyed the ship's main switchboard which delayed her delivery for several weeks.

On delivery she was employed cruising in the Caribbean and also out of Vancouver to Alaska during the summer. She was used as a hotel ship during the 2000 Summer Olympics in Sydney and at the end of the Games she sailed to San Francisco and was renamed **Patriot** in 2000. Her first cruise commenced on 2 December 2000, sailing from San Francisco to Honolulu. Later the following year American Hawaii Cruises was declared bankrupt and she was laid up in Honolulu. She was later repossessed by Holland America Line, and in 2002 she was operating as **Spirit** for Louis Cruise Lines, then sub-chartered to Thomson Cruises in 2003, becoming **Thomson Spirit**.

In the background to the left is Radio City Tower, opened by Her Majesty Queen Elizabeth II in 1969. It is 138 metres high.

Vision of the Seas 1998   78,717gt.   2,050 passengers.   279 x 32.2 x 7.8m.   22 knots.
b. Chantiers de l'Atlantique, St Nazaire, France.   Yard No F31.   IMO 9116876

Royal Caribbean International
Vision of the Seas leaving the Cruise Terminal on a bright summer evening.

Voyager   1990   15,396 gt.   520 passengers.   150.7 x 19.8 x 5.7m.   18.8 knots. b. Union Naval de Levante, Valencia, Spain.   Yard No 185.   IMO 8709573

Voyages of Discovery

Built as **Crown Monarch** for Crown Cruise Lines to cruise in the South Pacific and the Caribbean. She was chartered for use as a casino ship by Singapore interests in 1995, becoming **Nautican**. She was renamed **Walrus** when she moved to Hong Kong and was then laid up until she was sold to Club Cruiser in 2006, and chartered to Vision Cruceros as **Jules Verne**. In 2008 she was operating as **Alexander Von Humbolt II**. However, when the company was placed into administration she was laid up at Bremerhaven and sold in 2009 to the All Leisure Group, chartered to Phoenix Reisen. In 2012 she became **Voyager** and is seen on an evening departure from the Mersey.

Waverley

1947
693 gt.
925 passengers
73 x 17m.
14 knots
b. A&J Inglis Limited,
Glasgow.
Yard No 1330P
IMO 5386954

Waverley Steam Navigation Company

Waverley berthing at the landing stage at Liverpool to embark passengers for a cruise to Llandudno and Menai Bridge, North Wales.

Following the nationalisation of Britain's railways in 1948 the Scottish steamers, of which *Waverley* was one, became the responsibility of the Caledonian Steam Packet Company. On 1 January 1973 the Caledonian Steam Packet merged with David MacBrayne becoming Caledonian MacBrayne Limited.

Waverley was withdrawn from service in 1973 and she was sold to the Paddle Steamer Preservation Society (PSPS) for the token sum of one pound. A public appeal secured funding to enable the PSPS to operate Waverley the paddler. Each year *Waverley* completes a programme of excursion sailings around the British Isles. She sails regularly from Glasgow and other towns on the Firth of Clyde, the Thames, the south coast of England and the Bristol Channel.

Waverley has been rebuilt and reboilered with money from the National Lottery Fund.